FESTIVALS OF CHINA'S ETHNIC MINORITIES

By Xing Li

CHINA INTERCONTINENTAL PRESS

图书在版编目（C I P）数据

中国少数民族节日：英文／邢莉编著；王国振等译．
北京：五洲传播出版社，2006.10（2007.8 重印）
（中国民族多元文化丛书）
ISBN 978-7-5085-0999-0

I．中… II．①邢…②王… III．少数民族－民族节日－中国－英文 IV．K892.1

中国版本图书馆 CIP 数据核字（2007）第 139420 号

FESTIVALS OF CHINA'S ETHNIC MINORITIES

撰　　文：邢　莉
图片提供：邢　莉、黄　泽、黄健民、韩连赟、刘扬武、李期博、李跃波、尼玛江才、黄燚红、李木易、黄金国、袁心海、李全举、高志勇、赵　亮、李建泉、向晓阳、张新军、张国军、苏　涛、李远新、黄金国、刘普礼、吴吉斌、秦　刚、张天林、周志刚、周卫林、许云华、鲍利辉、文　林、吴柏松、萧云集、张　欣、程　洁、刘鸣亮、曹志政、焦　波、贾福明、尹恩彪、吴东俊、王平平、李远新、彭　年、王天抒、王玉山、宋红梅、Guang Niu
英文翻译：汉　定、王国振
责任编辑：徐醒生
编　　辑：何　云
装帧设计：孙思宇
出版发行：五洲传播出版社（北京海淀区莲花池东路北小马厂 6 号　邮编：100038）
网　　址：www.cicc.org.cn
印　　刷：北京嘉彩印刷有限公司
开　　本：787 × 1092 毫米　1/16
印　　张：8
版　　次：2006 年 10 月第一版　第一次印刷　2009 年 4 月第三次印刷
印　　数：3001 — 5000
书　　号：ISBN 978-7-5085-0999-0

定　　价：68.00 元

CONTENTS

CONTENTS

CONTENTS

Preface

The People' s Republic of China is a great multi-ethnic tapestry composed of 56 ethnic groups each with their own culture, traditions and festivals. The sheer variety and color of this old Chinese festival culture is truly mind-boggling. Every month of the year sees the celebration of one or more ethnic festivals. The celebrations and festivals peculiar to each ethnic group influences the celebrations and festivals of other groups but yet amid all this tumult; amid all the homogenizing forces of modern existence, each manages somehow to preserve their own unique voice and flavor.

Traditional ethnic festivals everywhere are an expression of a community's social, economic and cultural life and all gradually evolve with the changing circumstances of history: changes which manifest themselves in terms of the lifestyle, historical traditions, and religious and psychological beliefs of individual ethnic groups.

Traditionally the celebration of festivals among the various cultures that make up the human species is closely related to nature: to the changing seasons, the exigencies of agriculture and harvesting and the changing climatic conditions that each season brings. The traditional Chinese calendar, the lunisolar calendar, takes the period of time the moon takes to go from full to full as one month. The first day of the lunar month is known as Shuori, and the fifteenth day is called Wangri, One year, as in the western calendar, is composed of twelve months but there are 30 days in a large month and 29 days in a small month. Thus the lunisolar year has 11 days fewer than the solar tropical year.

Some ethnic groups follow the Han calendar, but some have their own calendars. Many pastoral festivals are held at times dictated by an ethnic group's own view of time and season. The Kazaks, who use their own ancient Kazak calendar, hold their Spring Festival, called the "Nawoluz Festival" on the vernal equinox of the Chinese lunar calendar. Daytime and nighttime are equal on the Vernal Equinox, so Kazaks take it as New Year's Day: "New Year sets in" is the literal translation of "Nawoluz". The calendar of the Khalkhas is based on a division of time into twelve year cycles, each symbolized by a different animal. The eleventh day of the first month of the lunar year, which is the second day after the first time the Aries Star appears to the south, is celebrated as the Khalkha Spring Festival.

Sinkiang Yingerle Mongolia Autonomous Prefecture and Bortala Mongolia Autonomous Prefecture hold a Zulu Festival, on October 25 by the Mongolian Calendar which they regard as Midwinter, calling it "the day the sun comes back" (the Mongolian Calendar is one month behind the lunar calendar), and the herders who live here take this

date as the date by which they calculate their age.

The character of the festivals and the way in which they come into being is closely related to the natural environment and the mode of production of individual ethnic minorities. For example in Mongolia and Tibet, where animal husbandry is the dominant way of life, you find festivals such as the Thriving Livestock Breeding Festival, the Sheep Herding Festival, the Little Horse Festival and the Horse Milk Festival. The Kazaks, Mongolians and Tibetans have always relied greatly on horses so it is no surprise to see these cultures celebrating regular horse racing festivals. Ethnic groups like the Tong, Miao, Bai, Gelao and Naxi on the other hand engage principally in the cultivation of rice and so they celebrate events like the Tasting Fresh Festival, which is held when the harvest is approaching and expresses the people's expectation of the harvest and their appreciation of the hard work that will involve. The torch festivals celebrated by ethnic groups such as the Yi, Gelao, Naxi and Bai groups is an expression of the importance of driving out insects, an element extremely important to their respective farming cultures.

A festival's origin also relates to the religious beliefs of a particular ethnic group. In primitive society, religion in essence came into being in response to people's awe towards and fear of nature. Many ethnic festivals owe their origins to the beliefs of these primitive religions. All traditional Chinese festivals: Spring Festival, Yuanxiao Festival, the Pure Brightness Festival, Dragon Boat Festival, Mid-autumn Festival and Chongyang Festival have emerged today from ancient primitive rituals.

Many Tibetan festivals originate from the concept that every single thing on earth has a soul. To take three examples the Harvest Festival is an expression of adoration for the Land Goddess, the Mountain Strolling Fair originates from reverence for the Mountain God and the Arrow Inserting Festival from worship of the arrow. The origin of the torch festivals held by many ethnic groups is the common primitive worship of fire. Many religions focus on the belief that all people have souls, and this gives rise to the ancestor worship, which is such a common feature of Chinese society even today. Many ethnic festivals came into being because of ancestor worship: the belief that reverence and respect is due to the ancestors of one's own family and tribe.

Modern religious beliefs also enrich Chinese festival culture. Many Tibetan and Mongolian herders replaced or merged their ancient religious beliefs with Buddhism in the period between the seventh and thirteenth century. Thus colorful folk cultures blend with traditional Buddhist Festivals to produce unique cultural mergings, which, because of the wide participation of the people, are not only confined to the temples, but burst out and become a vital expression of the character of people's everyday existence. According to statistics, there are as many as 50 Tibetan Buddhist Festivals with such origins. Broadly speaking they can be broken down into three categories: the first is celebrations associated with the dates of the birth and death of the primary Buddhas such as Sakyamuni, Tsong-kha-pa, Apothecary Buddha, Buddha Maitreya, and Lotus Flower Master; the second is to do with ritualized temple activities and taboos such as Free Captive Animals Festival, Six-four Festival, Rewarding Deities Festival, Grand Buddha Respecting Festival, Bathing Festival, Seventh-month Great Warrior Attendants Festival; the third is related to the Dharma Meetings held by the Lamas in the temples which grew into festivals when such meetings became large-scale gatherings. The Hui, Kazak, Uygur, Khalkhas, Uzbek, Tatar, Dongxiang, Bonan, Salar, and Tajik peoples are predominantly Moslem. They celebrate the Corban Festival and Eid, the Festival of Fast-breaking according to the teachings of Islam.

Some festivals owe their origins to ethnic folklore. The legends associated with events such as the Torch Festival, Water-splashing Festival, Tasting Fresh Festival, Sword-ladder Festival and Danu Festival go back to the age of myth. Those who participate do so just as their ancestors did in bygone centuries - as religious leaders, as representatives of heroes of legend and as respected community members. The origin of the Chinese traditional festival, the Dragon Boat Festival lies in the story of the great patriot, Qu Yuan. The legend of the founder of the Gelug Sect of Tibetan Buddhism, Tsong-kha-pa, is one of the sources of the Tibetan Ghee Lantern Festival. The Horse Races held in Lhasa on April 15 each year originate from a Tibetan Legend, which tells the story of the Tang Dynasty princess Wencheng arriving in Tibet to be married to the Tupan leader, Songtsan Gampo. Legend has it the race was first held by him to welcome Princess Wencheng.

The particular cultural psychology of the individual ethnic groups is also a vital factor one must consider if one wishes to trace the origins of certain festivals.

Traditional agricultural society is almost wholly dependent upon an abundant harvest each year and the wellbeing of its livestock and poultry for its survival. Thus in almost all agricultural cultures the concept of passing time and of ritual and celebration is inextricably linked with the growing period of crops. The planting and reaping of crops forms an unbreakable link in the chain of societal survival and so is of intrinsic importance to the culture of the group.

As the *Guliang Legend* records, "All the food crops ripen at harvest time; when abundant crops are completely ripe it means a bumper harvest." Many prayers for the coming year are made by women during the respective Spring Festivals of each ethnic group: the Gelao and Chuang shoulder new water on the first day of the first month of the lunar year; the Tong have the custom of "Singing the Eldest Sister" with the eldest girl being sung to by her siblings to pray for the success of the coming year's harvest and marriages. Prayers for the coming year are also important for each ethnic group in terms of planting in spring and harvesting in autumn. Not only can one find such prayers among crop-growing groups, it is also evident among stock-raising groups. Certain differences do, however, manifest themselves between the two groups in accordance with their

differing imperatives. The flight from the land to the cities: a mass migration of people whose scale exceeds any in previous history, has had a great impact on ethnic groups once wholly dependent on keeping animals. It means that festivals such as the Livestock Festival and Shepherd Festival are today in grave danger of extinction. In traditional society affluence was measured in terms of livestock; these days wealth is measured in the consumer goods of urban existence.

Human civilization has always had as one of its central focuses reproduction. Reproduction means survival. To ensure the survival of one's tribe, the rites of marriage and birth are of vital importance. In feudal society, arranged marriages were very much the norm. Loveless marriages were typical. The Qi Qiao Festival on the seventh day of the seventh month of the lunar year, the Mid-autumn Festival and Sisters Festival of many ethnic groups all owe their origins to the desire for love and free marriage. In traditional society, because of the lack of technological sophistication, manual labor is the driving force behind the community's productivity, and also very often the sole means by which one may acquire wealth. More hands meant more productivity. Thus the emphasis in traditional society was very much on giving birth to as many children especially boys as possible. These ideas are reflected very clearly in many ethnic festivals.

Wealth, the ability to produce male children and longevity are all traditionally seen as the very exemplars of good fortune. Though China's ethnic groups are widely distributed all over the land and their various festivals are each imbued with their own individual characteristics the concept of praying for good fortune and asking for blessing permeate every festival and indeed could be said to form an underlying foundation of China's rich and colorful festival culture. The Sisters Festival of the Hani originates from the legend that a girl refused what she saw as an unsuitable marriage and in the end died for love; the Butterfly Fair of Dali comes from a story that a pair of star-crossed lovers became butterflies; the Nianxi Flower Festival of Manchu originates from a tale that a beautiful girl was burned into ashes by the Fire-demon, her ashes then scattering on the land where they became nianxi flowers. The commemoration of the hero or heroine in the legends expresses a common desire to break away from the bondage of some restrictive traditional customs.

China is one of the world's great ancient civilizations with a history of some 5,000 years. Celebrations and festivals are an intrinsic part of that civilization. Some festivals have been held continuously for over 2,000 years. The festivals are important sources of cultural expression and enjoyment not only for Chinese people, but also for neighboring Asian countries and for expatriate Chinese communities around the world. Indeed one could confidently say that Chinese festival culture is now an intrinsic part of global heritage and culture.

CHAPTER I CHINESE NEW YEAR

The New Year in China is the most important and the most ceremonious festival of the year. These celebrations have a number of unique attributes.

The New Year has been celebrated by the Chinese people for over three millennia. No matter where a Chinese person should find him or herself at this time of year, Chinese New Year will be celebrated with tremendous earnestness. It is not only among the Han people that Chinese New Year is celebrated. Practically all the ethnic minorities also have the custom of celebrating this important festival. However, in different regions, ecological environments, and societies, the New Year is celebrated in different ways and at different times.

The New Year for the Han ethnic group is also called the Spring Festival because this is the first festival of spring in the new year. Spring Festival is also celebrated by 38 other minorities, making a total of 39 ethnic groups according to *A Complete Edition of Chinese Ethnical Festivals*. Among 31 of these ethnic societies all the people celebrate the festival, namely the Han, Manchu, Korean, Hezhen, Mongolian, Daur, Ewenki, Oroqen, Tu, Yugur, Xibe, Pumi, Qiang, Yi, Bai, Hani, Lisu, Naxi, Jingpo, Achang, Nu, Miao, Dong, Shui, Gelao, Zhuang, Yao, Jing, Li, and She. Among the other 8 ethnic groups only some people celebrate this festival. They are the Hui, Dongxiang, Tujia, Maonan, Wa, Mulam, Dai, and Kirgiz.

The Spring Festival is also observed in some Southeast Asian countries, due to the pervasive historical influence of China on her neighbors

I.New Year Celebrations in Northeast and Northwest Chinese Minorities

Seven ethnic groups have traditionally lived for countless generations in the regions of Northeast China and Inner Mongolia. The territory from the Loess Plateau and the Inner Mongolian Plateau to the Hun Lunbei'er Grassland is the cradle of the Mongolian people; the Daxing'anling and Xiaoxing' anling Mountains are the main areas where live the Ewenki and Oroqen peoples; the area around the Changbaishan Mountain and the Heilongjiang River is the heartland of the Manchu and the Daur ethnic groups; the Hezhen people who live by fishing are concentrated on the Sanjiang Plain (the alluvial plain formed by the Heilongjiang, the Songhua, and the Wusuli Rivers); meanwhile on the banks of the Hailanjiang River there live the Korean ethnic group where the cultivation of rice dominates society. According to their different cultures and ways of life, different ways of celebrating the New Year have sprung up among these communities.

The White Festival of Mongolians

The Mongolian people live on the boundless grasslands that stretch across their land. For them, the New Year is a long festival, which they call the "White Festival". People on this grassland place great reverence on the color white. White stands for purity, prosperity, holiness and happiness in their traditions. The designation is derived from the fact that people of all ages and both sexes in the Yuan Dynasty would traditionally put on white clothes on New Year's Day as this day was the beginning of the white month (i.e., the first month). White clothes are thought to be greatly auspicious.

The New Year celebrations among the Mongolians are divided into the Lesser New Year and the Great New Year.

When celebrating the Lesser New Year, people offer sacrifice to the Fire and Kitchen Gods. Such sacrifices have a long history, going back to the very beginnings of Shamanism and Lamaism, which comes from the holy word "Lhamo" coined by Padmasambhava. Before this sacrificial ceremony, people first clean their homes (called gers), their cooking utensils and set up the Huochengzi (a traditional Mongolian cooking range). In some regions the Huochengzi is even decorated with colored ribbons. Blue and white ribbons represent the blue sky and white clouds; yellow and red strips are tokens of Kagyupa and Gelugpa; and green symbolizes plants. Sacrifices include mutton, pig's large intestines, tea, butter, milk wine, Chinese dates etc. As the ceremony begins, the family members led by their patriarch begin to burn joss sticks, chant scriptures and offer sacrifices unto the fires, at the same time making congratulatory and imprecatory speeches in Mongolian and Tibetan. Very interestingly, during these addresses, the master chants: "Come near, good fortune. Good fortune, come near" while wielding an auspicious arrow. It's said that the Mongolians living in the eastern regions still observe the custom of throwing food into fires during the New Year celebrations.

Traditional Mongolian celebrations also include many customs of worshipping the Buddha and paying respect to one's ancestors. Several days before the Great New Year, women begin to prepare a great feast. Mongolians traditionally love fried food with flour, and also sweet mutton dishes. Besides fragrant and sweet fried food, food made in various ways from milk, such as Mongolian Cheese and Mongolian Butter Cheese are also extremely popular. These are called white foods by natives.

On the 29th day of the 12th lunar month, people place offerings before images of the Buddha and their ancestors, and light joss sticks and kowtow. Many Mongolian peoples also have the custom of worshipping Heaven. But this is done at different times in different places. It falls on the night of the 30th day of the 12th month in some regions, on the evening of which Mongolians toss successive cups of wine towards the sky and down to the earth, out of respect for Heaven and for their ancestors. Herdsmen in some pastoral areas will pile up a so-called "Tengger Aobao" with cow dung for kowtowing and praying. They believe the New Year is the common festival of both men and nature; their creed is no nature, no life.

Mongolian boiled lamb is absolutely essential for New Year's Eve. Usually prepared and eaten without any seasoning, the Mongolian boiled lamb is cooked by putting an entire slaughtered lamb into a large cauldron and then boiling it until it's seventy or eighty percent cooked. The eating of the lamb is quite ritualized. The whole cooked lamb is placed on an enormous platter, its hind legs both stretched out, the two front legs folded, with the head resting on top of them. The crooked horns and intact head of the beast about to be eaten will surely give you a vivid impression of the cultural continuity of this once nomadic, tribal people. Old and young sit around and cut off chunks of meat using elegant knives. When having a meal, herdsmen pay great attention to formalities: young men must toast their elders while the elders bestow sincere blessings on the young people. On the night of New Year's Eve, the far-reaching and melodious strains of the traditional Mongolian instrument, the Ma Tou Qin will be heard echoing from warm gers through the night sky; and a festive mood fills the whole grassland.

Mongolians lay great emphasis on paying New Year visits. If these are to the elder members of their family, they will ride galloping horses (often these days motorbikes). When carrying out these formalities, they make presents of snow-white hada and mellow wine to show their respect. The intoxicating songs which accompany the drinking of wine give the people a great sense of optimism and courage as they face into the life of another new year.

The Manchu Spring Festival Celebrations

The Manchu people are traditionally divided into red, yellow, blue, and white banners. During the Spring Festival, the people of each banner will proudly hang up their respective banner. For example, the people of the red banner paste red banners. These bright and beautiful banners are seen as guarantees of a propitious beginning to the new year.

The Manchu also have a strong tradition of ancestor worship. Traditionally enshrined on the west wall of Manchu residences was an "Ancestry Board". For this reason it is forbidden to sit on the west kang.

During a meal, it's customary for the elders and guests to eat first and the women and youngsters later. After the women and daughters-in-law carefully set the table, arranging the bowls, the chopsticks and the dishes, the diners then sit around the dining table on the kang and begin to eat. At this time, daughters-in-law will respectfully stand aside, ready to bring more rice and dishes to the menfolk and guests.

When the festival comes, gangs of Manchu boys take great delight in riding on various self-made ploughs to go to see relatives and friends. From the first to the fifth day of the first lunar month, the traditional yangko dance is performed in all Manchu areas. Some well renowned yangko performers perform not only in their own villages but also in neighboring regions. These merry dances carry people joyfully into the new year.

New Year Celebrations for the Daur People

The Daur people inhabiting the Nenjiang River valley customarily paste New Year pictures and Spring Festival scrolls around their homes. Several decades ago, the couplets on these scrolls were written in Mongolian, but many now appear in Chinese. Whatever the script, the message is one of prayers for good fortune and longevity for the new year. These scrolls are pasted on cabinets and boxes. The Door-god pictures are pasted on the gates and doors of residences and storehouses. The Daur also heap jumbles of grass and dried cow dung together into piles. When the veil of night falls, the heaps will be set alight one after another. At this time, the dancing flames and wisps of smoke illuminate the great festive mood. The Daur hold that the fires are a link with the fires of previous years, which symbolizes the prosperity of the family and the continuity of their society.

On the first day of the first month, the Daur people have the habit of rising early. Youngsters are urged to wake up by themselves: the Daur think in this way the young will grow into independent and diligent adults. Elders of the family lay the table in the courtyard and place upon it sacrifices such as meat, wine, or sweetmeats. All the family members burn joss sticks and kowtow to Tengger (the Heaven), Triones, the Niangniang Goddess, and the Kitchen God, praying for their blessing and a peaceful year and a bountiful harvest. Afterwards, they return to the house. The youngsters say to the elders: "Long may you live!" and the elders in return wish the youngsters happiness and the diligence necessary to be successful. The New Year breakfast is dumplings boiled with broth. Breakfast eaten, people ride horses, big-wheeled carts or ploughs to pay New Year visits to their relatives and friends.

During this period, many entertainments are held. Boys in groups play hockey; little girls gather to make and play with toys; local actors chant epics till the dawn. By the time of the Lantern Festival, which falls on the fifth day of this month, entertainment activities reach a peak.

The Noruz of the Kazakh

Noruz is New Year's Day for the Kazakh people. It falls on the vernal equinox according to the lunar calendar. The celebration of the festival at this time is determined by centuries of tradition and life. The old Kazakh people lived a nomadic life on the vast grassland. Where there were waters and grass, there were Kazakh people. Each time when winter would fall, livestock would be enclosed in pens next to warm cabins in which the long and cold season would be passed. By the spring, the livestock would be driven out to the hillsides where the ice and snow would be beginning to melt, and the nomadic seasonal life cycle would begin once more.

However the day on which the livestock would be driven out was really hard to select. Sometimes they would arrive at the hillsides only to be met with an abrupt drop in temperature and many of their sheep and goats would die, as there was no pasture for them to feed on. Afterwards, a wise old man formulated a rule that if the livestock were driven out after the vernal equinox, such calamities would occur no longer. In order to celebrate this major discovery, people gathered in Grandmother Noruz's to celebrate. Grandmother Noruz boiled seven kinds of food like rice, millet, milk lumps, horseflesh and kernels, into a porridge, which ever after became known as Noruz Porridge. Since then, people will celebrate the vernal equinox every year and Noruz Porridge is an absolute necessity. Besidesthis porridge, other delicacies are also served, such as the large intestines of horses and sausages made from horse ribs. During the festival, people firstly offer the heads of lambs to the old men, who in turn bestow their blessings and congratulations. The other people just listen quietly smiling happily. Then, with great joy, they tuck into their portion of Noruz Porridge. It is an event of enormous significance for the Kazakh people to have their New Year meal with their relatives and the elderly. They believe the new is generated by the old; the old is the mother while the new is the infant.

Another school of thought contends that the word " Noruz" is transliterated from the ancient Turkic language, which means "new". So the festival is used for celebrating the time when the nomads leave the cabins, and go to the grassland to begin the new year' s nomadic life. The preparation and eating of Noruz Porridge is to pray for a good harvest in the coming year. Whatever one believes about the origin of the word 'noruz', what matters is the earnest wishes the word represents. As winter turns to spring, Noruz is a carnival celebrating the continuity of life. People sing Noruz songs and play traditional instruments, and engage in wrestling contests.

Noruz of the Kirgiz

Noruz is also the New Year of the Kirgiz people. They designate the 11th day of each year's first month, namely the second day after the Aries constellation first appears in the sky in the south, as their New Year' s Day. Before the festival, people diligently clean their homes and prepare the special New Year food-Keque, which is made of flayed barley and wheat, vegetable oil, beef and mutton, onion, raisins etc. During the festival, every family presents delicacies and good wine to cater for friends that come to pay New Year calls. They will sing and dance, race horses and wrestle on the vast grassland. By the time night comes, when livestock come back from the pasture, each family kindles a heap of splendid achnatherum before their yurt. First the people and then the livestock will jump over it, indicating the elimination of disasters and the prosperity of both the family members and the livestock that will surely come in the new year.

II.New Year Celebrations Among Some Ethnic Groups in Southwest China

Many ethnic minority groups live in the southwest areas of China. And many of them have the custom of celebrating the New Year.

The Tibetan New Year

The Tibetans living in Tibet and Qinghai Province celebrate the New Year according to the Tibetan calendar. As early as 100 BC, the Tibetan people began to calculate time according to the wax and wane of the moon. The New Year's Day at that time fell roughly on what is today the first day of the 11th month in Tibetan calendar. From 1027, the Tibetans began to adopt what is referred to as the Tibetan calendar, using the ten Heavenly stems and the twelve Earthly Branches matched with the Five Elements to calculate the passing of days. In this unique calendar 60 years constitutes one complete cycle. However the day on which Tibetan New Year falls varies in different Tibetan areas. In regions like

Lhasa it falls on the first day of the first Tibetan month.

The Tibetan people have the custom of making a "Qiema" box during the New Year. The method is to put into each side of an elegant quadrate box, barley kernels and zanba (a Tibetan food mixed with ghee), with Qingke spikes and beautiful molded flowers covered in ghee. The Qiema box is also painted beautifully using colored ghee, usually featuring such figures which represent longevity and harmony. The Tibetans take Qiema as a mascot; barley kernels are a token of good luck; and zanba symbolizes health and a bountiful harvest for the new year.

The Tibetans pay great attention to cleaning their cooking ranges. They sprinkle some zanba flour on the middle wall and fashion it into an "Auspicious Eight-Figure Emblem". And on the gates and walls they draw representations of the ears of highland barley with white lime and lacquer. Some are auspicious designs, representing the prosperity of the family and the value of grain. The Tibetans also hang Tangka paintings and offer sacrifices. They usually make the portraits of their forefathers that have passed away into Tangka and hang them out together with other beloved Buddha Tangka paintings. Before these figures, they will place some offerings like lumps of ghee, milk tea, and candies. Meanwhile, they light their ghee lamps to show their respect for the Buddha and also for their ancestors.

Mutton, ghee tea and chang comprise the typical dishes for the Tibetan New Year. On the 29th day of the 12th Tibetan month, people first eat the "Gutu" soup, which is made of nine ingredients, including fried meat, carrots, Chinese cabbage, sapodilla plums, and peas. Most interestingly everyone has to eat at least nine bowls. The cook deliberately puts stones, wool, pepper, wood charcoal and other items into the soup. The one who comes upon the pepper is thought to be locquacious; the wool stands for a good heart while on the other hand, the wood charcoal is a token of a black heart.

At night, people begin the ritual of "sending off ghosts". They firstly use straw to fashion nine crisscrossed figures to represent ghosts. They then put leftover food and cloth, and some money into a shabby gallipot. The next step is to send off ghosts at night, the later, the better, lest ghosts in other homes should come in. when the ceremony is being performed. The inside and outside of the house is thoroughly smoked using a lit torch; then some zanba is scattered on the ground; and at last, the straw ghost figures are taken out. The whole family escorts them to a field far away from their residence in order to bring good fortune for the coming year.

On the morning of the first day of the year, the Tibetans get up very early. They rush off in order to bring back the first bucket of water, which is seen as being most auspicious.

All the family members sit together to enjoy a meal made of sapodilla plums, ghee and sugar. After that, the master takes out the five-cereal cup. Everyone puts a few cereals into their mouth and makes a prayer of best wishes after offering some grain to the gods. From the second day on, people begin to pay New Year calls. The master prepares Qiema to honor guests. Before taking zanba, the guests must firstly offer it to the heavenly and earthly gods. Afterwards, they begin to drink and sing and enjoy various entertainments.

The New Year Customs of Other Minorities

The minority ethnic groups living on the Yunnan-Guizhou Plateau also celebrate the New Year. Some like the Hani and the Yi celebrate two New Years and some even three New Years. For example, the Hani people celebrate the New Year in both the sixth and the tenth months. However, the Drung ethnic group in previous years because of extreme poverty would only celebrate New Year once every three years. The timing of the various New Year celebrations also varies from ethnic group to ethnic group. For some it is in the first lunar month; for some in the fourth or fifth month, and some in the tenth month. The Lisu celebrate the New Year in the 12th month when the wild cherry blossoms unfold. The dates of the New Year for the Nu people vary in different regions. Some celebrate around January 1 and some follow the practice of the Han.

Many of the Southwest minority ethnic groups preserve the custom of offering sacrifice but various beliefs accompany these sacrifices. The Nu people, who live in the area of the Bijiang River, Yunnan, perform the ceremonies of Ruwei and Kuabai. Ruwei relates to worship of the corn god and is held on the 29th day of the 12th lunar month. The participants are all adult men. “Kuabai” means knocking the plough. When this rite is carried out on the eve of the New Year, the master of ceremonies takes the lead in knocking the ploughshare. And then the others in turn follow his lead. The purpose is to pray to the Rain God for rain.

The grandest activity for the Drung people during the New Year is “offering an ox to the heavens”. The ox is offered either by one family or by the community. The clan leader or the master who presides over the annual sacrifice firstly decorates the ox with plenty of glistening beads on its horns and a glorious Drung blanket on its back and then fastens it to a post in the center of the square. The master of ceremonies then lights pine torches facing the east, in order to worship the Mountain God. At the end, the beads and blanket are taken off the ox. Then two hunters come into the arena from opposite sides, with bamboo spears in their hands. The surrounding people take their turns to toast them. The two drink heavily and dance intensely. At that time, with the sound of the bronze gongs

ringing all around, all the surrounding people begin to perform the Intrepid Ox Dance. The two hunters jump to either side of the ox and thrust their spears into the ox. Other people hand in hand wield knives and bows, shouting at the ox until it finally falls down dead. Victorious laughter runs through the crowd. At once they cut up the ox into many pieces and boil them right away in a great pot. Everyone present will get their portion. The people eat the meat while dancing, praying fervently for a good harvest in the coming year.

A lot of ethnic groups, such as the Dong and the Miao, still today perform the Lu Sheng Dance.

The Dong people are famous for singing and dancing. They use a wind instrument named Lu Sheng, which is made by fixing several giant reeds on a wooden pedestal. Lu Shengs are all of different lengths. The shortest one is only two *chi* high (3*chi*=1 meter) whereas the longest is as high as three meters. However, in spite of their different lengths, all Lu Shengs have six reed pipes and five tones. It produces a most sweet-sounding music. In some areas when playing the Lu Sheng, the Lu Sheng players often put on Duijin garments (a kind of Chinese-style jacket with buttons down the front) made of Dong cloth; they wrap their heads in a black scarf which then is fashioned into the shape of a chignon.

For the Dong people, the New Year is a carnival. At that time, the performances of the fully dressed up Lu Sheng players attract all the people of the village to the local meeting place. As the ceremony begins, an old man of noble character and high prestige blows first into the Lu Sheng and dances before other people enter the field to join him in the dance. With Lu Sheng in their hands, the players dance along to various cadenced melodies. Their steps vary according to the rhythms: sometimes steady, sometimes vehement and sometimes slow. They dance alone or in groups. On this day, the girls are especially beautiful. They put on black costumes made of Dong cloth, and coil their hair into great projecting chignons. Offsetting their black costumes, their heads are decorated with various silver flakes and the feathers of pheasants dyed pink. Three, four or five rings of silver ornaments adorn their necks; precious lockets lie upon their bosoms; and around their waists are embroidered geometrical patterns dotted with shining silver pendants. It is indeed a dazzlingly beautiful and colorful costume. This festival is seen a very propitious occasion for girls to find their lovers.

"Dancing Flower" or "Dancing on the Flower Field" is a festival celebrated by the Miao people living in Guizhou, Anshun, and Qiannan in Guizhou Province. It is held on a selected day from the first day of the first lunar month and usually lasts two or three days. During this period, people play the Lu Sheng, dance Lu Sheng Dances and sing antiphonally on a field full of flowers, just outside the village. A flower post is erected by a selected host who at the same time chants in the Miao language. The post then is hung with a piece of red cloth and a broadsword at about chest height. Afterwards the new host and his predecessor blow together the opening notes on the Lu Sheng, they lead a group of men playing the music while completing three laps around the post. This is the ceremonial representation of the beginning of the dance.

According to T*he General Annals of Guizhou-Records of Aboriginal Inhabitants of the Qing Dynasty*, "on the 11th, 12th, and 13th day of the first lunar month every year, the Miao people will dress up and find an open plain and plant a holly tree, which they name the "flower tree". With one end of cloth in their hands, the girls pull and drag each other while two young men dance and play the famous "male and female phoenix courting" melody. The girls move around the boys in a semicircle dancing all the while. This is called "dancing flower". After it finishes up on the 13th day, they let off fireworks and turn the 'flower tree' upside down. The girls select the young men they like and call him Lao Biao. Then with their Lao Biao's ribbon in their hands, they are led along by him." Today, the custom is that the girls follow the ribbon or towel of the men. This is called "pulling sheep".

"Treading Flower Mountain" is another New Year festival, which is common in Yunnan, western Guizhou and the Longlin area of Guangxi. Before this festival, a site is chosen and a 'flower tree' set up, signifying the immediate opening of the "flower mountain field". Passers-by will quickly pass on the news. In some areas, the flower pole is erected by a family who wishes to have a son. This festival also serves as an occasion when one can find a mate in these areas. Young boys and girls take the leading roles in the festival. A lad expresses his diligence and intelligence mainly through playing the Lu Sheng. And when dancing, if he finds a lively girl in the crowd, he just takes off his floral umbrella and swiftly opens it over her head. However, if the girl does not like this boy, she rushes off. If she likes him, she will stay under his umbrella. Then they find a retreat to express their mutual love and propose marriage. After they finally come to an arrangement, they will pay a visit to each other's parents at a specified time.

From the second day of the first lunar month, similar customs are observed by the Miao people inhabiting Gui'ding, Fuquan, Longli, and Kaiyang in Guizhou Province. This festival is called "Dancing the Moon", during which stockaded villages take turns to host the ceremony. The festivities again consist of Lu Sheng music, Ta-ge and dancing. With men playing the music at the front and ladies dancing to the tunes at the back, they circle the ground. Lovers convey their tender feelings via tying knots in each other's binds. The activity will last till the third night. In the past, when a field was newly used, the head of

the village would slaughter pigs to entertain guests while local families boiled sweet wine. Nowadays, the village whose turn it is to undertake the ceremony will prepare sweet wine, sticky rice cakes, preserved ham, sausages, and blood curd beforehand. Even strangers will be received warmly. The Lu Sheng players show their skills, and the most skilled and handsome attract the girls to dance behind them. The ceremony ended, young lads and girls invite acquaintances and old friends to accompany them to drink together in their homes. The revelry of the young boys and girls during the New Year represents the return of the god of life, and fulfils the twofold function of praying for a good harvest as well as finding a suitable mate.

III.The Celebration of New Year among Ethnic Groups in the South and Southeast of China

In the south and southeast areas of China live the Zhuang, Yao, Gelao, Bonan, Jing, Tujia, Li, She and Gaoshan ethnic groups. Though dotted with mountains, this is a largely wetland region featuring many paddy fields. The ancestors of the Zhuang - the Guyue people made an outstanding contribution to the development of the culture of rice cultivation.

The New Year Customs of the Zhuang Ethnic Group

The Zhuang people regard Spring Festival as the most important, most ceremonious festival of the whole year. After enjoying a sumptuous supper, the people stay up late or indeed all night on New Year's Eve sitting around the fire pit. When the first hour of the New Year arrives, firecrackers are let off, incense sticks and candles are lit and sacrifices such as pork, whole chickens, Zongzi, Tangyuan, and rice wine are offered in order to pay respect to the tribal ancestors. Zhuang women have the custom of drawing water from the mouth of the spring or the river in the New Year, believing that the fresh water brings them good luck. The men raise the lanterns and go to the temple to burn joss sticks and papers, praying for good fortune in the coming year.

The Zhuang observe many taboos on the first day of the new year: saying unlucky words; using scissors, for fear that the family will quarrel with each other in the new year; sweeping the floor, for fear of losing money; carrying things out of the house or even lending to others, for fear that such an action will presage fortune moving out of the house in the new year. It is forbidden in some places to beat drums and gongs in order not to startle the ghosts and gods. Most people of the group don't visit their neighbors at this time and it is also forbidden to kill living things and all pigs, chickens and ducks have to be killed and prepared several days before. People eat tangyuan at daytime and a meat dish for supper in the belief that it can eliminate disasters and diseases for the year ahead.

The custom of setting hardwood alight is also common in many Zhuang regions, and from the first to fifth day of the lunar new year, the fire cannot be allowed to go out. The smoke curling upwards signifies that the offspring will live long happy lives. From the second day of the New Year, the relatives and friends begin to pay New Year calls on each other. It is a time especially for married daughters to go back with husband and children to visit their mother's house with presents such as meat or chicken and duck. It is a great opportunity for married sisters to get-together and exchange news and gossip.

Among the Zhuang the first month of the New Year is regarded as a festival month. So the strong men of the Wenshan, Yunan beat drum and dance for one month. The young men in other areas hold singing contests or perform the famed lion dance, play Chongtang (usually called playing the shoulder pole - a kind of entertainment) and listen to the epics and dramas common to the Zhuang near the beautiful rivers or valleys which abound in these regions. Some areas such as He County in Guangxi Province also preserve the custom where the young men raise their self-made lanterns of various kinds and put on masks decorated like the ancients of the tribe to perform in neighboring villages. Such performances are a living, breathing cultural link between past and present.

Tujia Ethnic Minority New Year Celebrations

The Tujia Ethnic Group celebrate their New Year one day before the Han, that is on the 29th of the 12th month of the lunar calendar. The origin of this practice can be traced back to history. In 1554, in Ming Dynasty times, the frontier was invaded by Japanese pirates, so the ancestors of the Tujia went to fight to resist the invader. It was right at New Year when the military orders came, so the people couldn't wait for the normal New Year and so decided to celebrate one day early, getting together with their families before taking to the battlefield to defend their lands from foreign oppression.

For the New Year festivities the Tujia kill a pig, and prepare bean curd, zanba and sausage. All the families sit around a big fire, and stay up late or even all night on New Year's Eve, to welcome in the New Year.

Their typical celebratory singing and dancing activity is known as "Waving Hands", which includes "Big Waving Hands" and "Small Waving Hands", the latter being of smaller scale with the dancers dancing around a circle and imitating farming actions while waving their hands. In the past, almost all villages held " Small Waving Hands" dances and set up a "Waving Hands Hall". The "Big Waving Hands" is a larger scale activity, in which both military and farming actions are mimed while waving hands. The dances performed in Madi Village on Dragon Mountain in Hunan Province are famous far and near and have a long and distinguished history. On the day of "Waving Hands" dancing, all the young strong men in the villages near Madi Village carry arms and wear flowery bedcovers as "armour". They then run in great swarms to the "Eight Manito" Temple accompanied by the loud sound of firecrackers. On arrival there, they perform tai qi exercises and give skilful displays of swordsmanship before beginning the performance of the "Waving Hands" dance, which forms the climax of the Spring Festival celebrations of the Tujia people.

The New Year Celebrations of the She Ethnic Minority

The New Year celebrations of the She ethnic group are very much associated with the custom of worshiping fire. Big logs of dry firewood are burned in every family' s stove on the night of New Year' s Eve. This is called "the kindling for the second year", and the people usually stay up all night. In the first half of the night, they visit neighbors, relatives and friends to celebrate the festive season; later, they light fragrant candles and set off firecrackers to welcome in the New Year. Finally the whole family gets together to have the New Year Meal. The people in some places make maci, eating some and leaving the leftovers in the barn, which are then taken out after 15th night of the first lunar month. This practice is known as "eating with balance and moderation".

In the wee hours, the children run into the bamboo gardens to shake "mao bamboos". It is believed that the children will grow fast and tall if they shake the "mao bamboos" on the first day of the lunar New Year. Another custom common among She families in mountainous areas involves the men running around the houses clapping their bamboo castanets on the morning of the first lunar day in order to expel the gods of plague and eliminate diseases and disasters. Some eat rice with "sweet potato pieces", a reminder to never forget important matters -an important element of the New Year celebrations for some people.

The entertainments of the She people during the Spring Festival include antiphonal singing, climbing contests, playing swing and playing chicun. This is a traditional physical sport where many people form a circle in a barnyard while one person stands in the middle of the circle holding a stick, called "Chi"and in the other hand a piece of bamboo, called "Cun". The person in the circle hits "Cun" with "Chi" and those who catch the "Cun" outside the circle win the game, the winner then taking his or her place in the middle of the circle as the game begins again. The She are renowned for their singing, especially their vivid folk songs which tell the tales of the historical legends of the She people.

Everybody, man or women, or even guests passing through can compete in the climbing contest. Before dawn, the people gather at the foot of the mountain and as soon as the sun rises, the starting shot is fired and the competitors begin to climb the mountain, all striving to be the first and fearing to lag behind the others. The one who is first to get to the appointed place wins a silk banner. Some She also do some hunting at this time and enjoy a great dinner feast, the eating accompanied by lusty singing of folk songs. For the swinging, a swing is made of supple mao bamboo, as wide as the mouth of the bowl, and the ends are connected with wattles, so the whole becomes a circle on which one person can sit. With the elasticity of the mao bamboo and the change in one's center of gravity, one can swing up and down freely, if a little dangerously . During the festival, there is also a well-established tradition of letting off firecrackers when the people of the She make their New Year visits. The host thus knows the guests are about to arrive and has time to prepare his own fireworks to welcome them.

The eighth day of the first lunar month is the date when the She worship their ancestors and totems. It is said that one of the greatest of She ancestors, Panhu, was allowed to marry a princess because he helped the Emperor resist foreign aggression. He moved to live in the deep mountain with his princess after their marriage. The couple were said to have had three sons and one daughter - their sons' and son-in-law's family names being respectively Pan, Lan, Lei and Zhong. This clan eventually multiplied to become the She people.

On this day, all the male, female, old and young people with the same ancestors and family name gather in their own family name's ancestral temple of each village, and carry out the anciently established ancestor worship ceremony, the oldest man in the family leading the ceremonial rites. After the ceremony, the people go to have a "Taigong Meal" with their common family, where tea and warm wine must be generously offered in order to entertain the honored guests who share the same ancestors.

The New Year Traditions of the Yao People

The Yao ethnic minority in Xing'an County of northeast Guangxi province, always burn a special-grained wood on the night of New Year's Eve, believing it to be something that brings good luck.

After supper, everyone washes their face, and then uses a wood basin filled with hot water to wash their feet and wipe their knees, believing thereby that all their wishes for the next year may be realized. They then hang up lamps in the hall and inner rooms - both upstairs and downstairs, in the hope that they may "fill the house with gold and jade". The host also carries a large piece of wood about two meters long and eventually burns it in the stove. This piece of wood must not be crossed by anyone, for it creates the special "Harmonious Fragrance" on New Year's night for the Yao ethnic group. The reason they burn the special-grain wood is that it has almost the same pronunciation as the two Chinese characters "He" and" mu", which mean "harmoniously creating wealth". Thus every family burns this wood on New Year's Eve, hoping for harmony in their families, villages and among all the people. This is of vital importance, so whatever you do, do not cross over the piece of wood.

At the beginning of the New Year, when the cock crows and day breaks, the womenfolk sweep up all the detritus lying on the ground outside the door into bamboo dustpans which are then emptied outside the village accompanied by some mumbled prayers. This is also a custom of the Yao, called "sending off laziness". It is felt that if 'lazy' things such as twigs of firewood and grass are cleared away on the first day of the New Year, then the whole family will be better able to face the chores and trials of the New Year diligently. The hard-working Yao depend on their own toil and sweat to create a happy life and thus they seek to sweep laziness away from their doors. This differs markedly from many other ethnic groups including the Han, where no sweeping is carried out on New Year's Day as it is felt that to sweep on this day is to sweep away all the good fortune from one's home.

CHAPTER II FESTIVALS OF PRODUCTION

Food and sustenance is a primary requirement for all people. The centrality of a successful harvest or of good hunting to the wellbeing of ancient tribal communities gave rise to many religious beliefs and festivals. Festivals of production are mainly based on the conventions of agriculture, animal husbandry, fishing and hunting. Being such a vast land, China has a diversity of ecological environments, which support a wide spectrum of agricultural and productive cultures and thus the country is home to a dizzying selection of traditional festivals associated with these diverse practices. Prayers for a good harvest remain the main theme of these festivals of production.

I.Festivals to Celebrate the Harvest

Sanyuesan

Sanyuesan (the third-day-of-the-third-month festival of song), is celebrated by the Zhuang, Dong, Bouyei, Shui, Mulam, Maonan, and Miao peoples, and is a common traditional festival in the southern areas of China. Held on the third day of the third lunar month, this festival is a celebration to welcome the harvest. It integrates elements connected with courtship and praying for rain and a bountiful harvest: overall, the main purpose is to celebrate the resurrection of the god of life.

Sanyuesan, also known as the Gexu or Gepo Festival, as celebrated by the Zhuang,, is a traditional festival, which is very much focused on the collective desire for a bountiful harvest, and in a larger sense a life of harmony and contentment for the Zhuang people. There are several legends which are said to explain the ultimate origin of this festival: one explanation is that, as singing pleases the gods, and thus can help prevent disasters, the festival naturally developed into festivities based around the singing of songs. Another explanation is that it was founded in memory of Sister Liu, for the third day of the third lunar month is the day when she passed away; a third viewpoint contends that Sanyuesan serves as a memorial to a pair of young lovers who died for love.

Before this festival, the Zhuang people boil maple-leaves, day lilies, and March flowers in order to color sticky rice and dye boiled eggs red; the girls embroider handkerchiefs with floral patterns while young lads purchase such gifts as scarves and combs. As evening falls, the Zhuang people put on rich costumes and with food and gifts in hand, men and women, boys and girls gather together on hilltops, fields, grassy slopes and bamboo forests to sing together, the questions and answers of the antiphonal style ringing out across the night air. Youngsters enjoy a whole host of social activities, choosing mates or just dating sweethearts. In accordance with traditional customs, Sanyuesan lasts two or three days. After singing during the daytime, more follows at night. The night singing is called Yegexu (night song festival); it lasts from dusk until the sun comes up the next day. The Zhuang take this to represent "long love in a short night", but people also believe that the singer who ushers in the dawn's early light with his or her singing will find true love and a happy marriage. Besides the singing of antiphonal love songs, there are a number of other entertainments like the tossing of brocade balls, the bumping of red eggs, beating sticks etc. The eggs bumped by the young people are eggs dyed red in most places while in some places are found five-colored eggs, which are used for warding off evil and protecting against disasters.

In the stockaded villages of the Dong people surrounded by lakes and rivers and mountains, young people, dressed up in all their finery, go to Xu (fairs) on the third day of the third lunar month. They exchange presents and whisper the sweet language of love in each other' s ears. In some places, a game takes place: the lads pretend to steal something from the girls and the girls pretend to give chase. The chase culminates in a secret place where more passionate wooing takes place. In the past, some lads and girls sang antiphonal songs s as they gradually approached each other. When faced with a sincere, amorous boy, the girl often stays over night. Celibate young lads of the Dong villages in Baojing, Guizhou, will ask the objects of their affection for bamboo baskets, an important token of their love.

The Bouyei people living in Guizhou also celebrate Sanyuesan. Besides singing, dancing and courting during this festival, they also hold ceremonies to expel pests and to pray for a bountiful harvest. They think that a good singing performance not only can capture their lover' s heart but also can protect the community from attack by insect pests. The Bouyei people living around the area of Anlong have the custom of offering sacrifice to the Mountain God on the third day of the third month since they believe this day is his birthday and he will discharge grasshoppers to harm crops if he is not appeased in some way. Hence their sacrifice is effectively a prayer for his forbearance and blessing. Still in some areas male and female adults have the custom of "hiding in the mountains", which effectively means making love in the woods. The Bouyeis of Luodian County, Guizhou Province call Sanyuesan, the Maple-leaf Festival. Girls and daughters-in-law usually pin several green maple-leaves on their heads, which are a token of the vitality and lifeforce of spring.

A vital duality dominates the Sanyuesan festivities of the Li people, that is, love and harvest. Their legends tells of how at one time a great drought descended upon the land:

rivers were all dried up; seedlings were all scorched. A young lad named Ya Yin dreamed that a lark could relieve the drought. Indeed soon after he found the lark, which later turned into a dazzling girl, who promised Ya Yin that she would save the day. Ya Yin and the fairy tilled land during the day and sang, danced, and played music at night. The rains duly returned; drought left the land. But the evil head of the village was jealous and forbade the girl to sing and play instruments, even in a fit of temper burning the finely crafted instruments. Ya Yin and the girl became a pair of birds and flew away. The day they left was said to be the third day of the third month, which later becomes a traditional festival of the Li. Every year at this time, the Li people hold great sacrificial ceremonies, in the hope of ensuring a good rice harvest and successful hunting. Girls and lads sing in the antiphonal style and dance the Bamboo Dance.

The Rao Sanling Celebrations of the Bai

Similar to the Sanyuesan of some south ethnic minorities, the Rao Sanling of the Bai people in Dali is the holiday when they go sightseeing in spring before getting down once again to the busy work of farming. It is also the holiday when they perform ceremonies to pray for a good harvest before transplanting the rice seedlings.

Sanling means three holy temples, the Celestial Beings' City-the Jinkui Temple of Heaicheng, Xizhou, the Gods' City-the Shengyuan Temple of Qingdong village, and the Buddha's City-the Chongsheng Temple of Dali. So at Rao Sanling many people make a pilgrimage to the three temples, which are said to have a history of over 1,000 years dating back to the Nanzhao Period. From the 23rd day to the 25th day of the fourth lunar month every year, tens of thousands of young and middle-aged people of all villages congregate at the foot of Cangshan Mountain beside Erhai Lake. They put on their very finest costumes, and in thronging groups, stroll around "Sanling". Predictably the festivities also provide a wonderful opportunity for courtship as young men and women eagerly socialize.

In these three days, tens of thousands of people come together into one enormous group. They rise at dawn and spend the day, beating drums, singing songs and dancing on the road. Participants are free to join up with any team that catches their fancy. The leaders of the group must be a pair of old singers of the Bai ethnic group. These two hold a willow branch between them; each with a yak tail in the other hand: one is in charge of the singing while the other concerns himself with joking and flirting with the crowds, waving his handkerchief in the air. However the content of the performance varies according to the predilections and tastes of the performers. Walking, dancing, singing the Daben Melody, and humming the unique songs of the Bai, they march along the foot of the Cangshan Mountain. About ten people follow immediately behind the captains; they blow on flutes and suona or play yu-kin or trichord sanxian. Next come well known male and female antiphonal singers, followed by dozens of teams wielding Overlord Whips. As night falls, they remain in the woods or on the grassland before the temple singing and dancing all night till dawn. The pilgrimage finished, people gather in a seaside village-Majiu and then scatter after offering their sacrifice and singing and dancing in the temple which was built as the shrine of Emperor Jing and a princess of the Bonan ethnic group. During the harvest season, they use willow branches to pray for rain; and one of the reasons why men and women sing and dance is also to pray for a good harvest.

Machongling Festival of the Zhuang

The Machongling (frog) Festival is the festival celebrated by Zhuang farmers. Held in Hechi, Baise, Donglan, and Fengshan in Guang and taking place during Spring Festival, it involves frog-worship activities. Full of local flavor, this festival is one of the most ceremonious and ancient traditions for the local people.

The Machongling Festival is a day showing respect for the frog. A local legend tells of how long long ago, there lived a dutiful son named Donglin of the Zhuang ethnic group. When his mother died, the frogs outside wept in sadness. The son burned the frogs to death for fear of disturbing his mother's soul. The frogs' crying ceased, but the insect pests began to thrive. The harvest was lost and the people were thrown into a desperate situation. Donglin realized the error of his ways and urgently sought to make amends. He organized a lavish funeral for the frogs, and even brought frogs into his home to celebrate traditional festivals with him in the first month of every year.

The Zhuang people have engaged in farming since ancient times. Frogs can eat pests and therefore are essential for protecting crops. So they are taken almost as objects of veneration by the Zhuang. Besides, some tribes of the Zhuang once worshiped frogs as totems in the remote past. One can perhaps see this festival as a relic from that time.

When Spring Festival comes, people congregate spontaneously around the Machongling Pavilion to take part in the grand Machongling festival of song. The sequence runs as follows: firstly Machongling must be found, then mourned and at last buried. In between times the demanding frog god must also be danced with and sang to. These rites celebrate the harvest and offer prayers for favorable weather in the coming year.

On the first day of the first month, more than ten young men in rich costumes, beating

gongs and drums, go to the field to find hibernating frogs. The first frog found is honored as the representation of Machongling and a song is sung to celebrate the joyous occasion. Afterwards, another frog is selected from among the others. The pair of frogs is then conveyed to the Machongling Pavilion. After receiving prayers, the two frogs are beaten to death and their remains enclosed in a big bamboo tube. The man who found the first frog is dubbed "Lord Machongling". He is given the honor of presiding over that year's ceremonies.

From the second day to the fifth day, Lord Machongling pays New Year calls from door to door during the day, carrying Machongling and singing the ancient Machongling songs. Hosts will present the Machongling Girl with rice, money, colored eggs, glutinous rice dumpling mixed with meat etc. The visiting doesn't end until the sun sets in the west. The money collected is public money and the rice is public rice; the former is put aside to pay for a great common feast, which will be held during the festival while the latter is distributed to the local kids. At night, villagers gather at the Machongling Pavilion, to wake the dead frogs.

On the last day of the first month, all families slaughter chickens and ducks, and boil five-colored sticky rice. After lunch, all the villagers will escort the frogs to the cemetery. Before burial, Lord Machongling opens the casket of the previous year's Machongling to examine their skeletons. If they are golden, it indicates an auspicious year of favorable weather. But if they are gray or black, people should take some measures to prepare for natural disasters like drought or flood and burn joss sticks and offer prayers for a good harvest and peace in the community. Then young people from several villages offer sacrifices, beat brazen drums, perform the Machongling dance and sing Machongling songs in order to celebrate the harvest and pray for good weather next year. In this vivid and quite unique dance, most movements and postures imitate those of frogs.

The Tajik Chowar Festival

The Chowar Festival of Tajik is also a festival of production.

The Chowar Festival is a water-drawing festival —— "chowar" in the Tajik language means drawing water. Both crop cultivation and pasture require water; water is the very lifeline of the harvest. The Pamirs where the Tajik people live is very cold. In winters, mountain streams freeze; and if the people don't break the ice to draw the water when spring comes, they cannot till the land and plant their seeds. The Chowar Festival celebrates the successful drawing of water.

It is held during the Tajik month of spring (from March 22 to April 22). Before the festival, the Tajik people scatter soil on the surface ice of the rivers, which contributes to the melting of the ice. They prepare tools for breaking ice and bake three big pieces of Nang (a kind of pancake made of wheat or corn flour), with one being left at home and two carried to the water. When the festival begins, all villagers led by the Mulafu (water official) ride horses to the waterside to take part in the breaking of the ice and the construction and renovation of irrigation channels. As the water is directed into the channels, people sit together and enjoy their Nang while children frolic happily in the water. They all pray together for favorable weather and a good harvest. At last, they ride off together to celebrate the festival and hold raucous contests such as sheep snatching and horse racing.

II.Festivals Praying for Harvest

Torch Festival

The Torch Festival is held at different times by different ethnic groups, but generally take place on June 24 or 25 of the Chinese Lunar Calendar. Some also celebrate the festival on the 6th day of the 6th lunar month and on February or August 24 of the Chinese Lunar Calendar. The festival usually lasts for three days, although some celebrate for seven days or in some cases as long as half a month, but all ethnic groups will have finished the ceremonies by the time the harvest season approaches.

The most important element in a Torch Festival is of course the great torch itself. In the areas inhabited by the Bai and Yi Ethnic Groups of Dali in Yunnan Province, every time the Torch Festival draws near, every village constructs a huge torch, three or four zhang high——it can take as many as four people to hold it. The large torch is made using pine and cypress wood as its trunk with dry firewood and pine branches fastened outside layer upon layer, in many ways like a splendid pagoda. The top of the torch is decorated with a great whorl and long banners are attached, along with lotus flowers, five-colored burgees, and small chickens and ducks cooked with rice and flour. On the night of the festival, the huge burning torches in the various villages turn the sky red. Holding small torches, every villager walks from house to house and round the edges of the fields, beating drums all the while.

The Bai Ethnic group has the custom of playing a game with their torches. On the night of the festival, both men and women, hold a burning torch in their left hand and carry with them turpentine powder in a small satchel. They then throw the turpentine on to other people' s torches, thus causing enormous bursts of fire to rear up from their neighbor' s

torches. Despite what seems a very dangerous activity, it is regarded by locals as a kind of friendly gesture. The people think that the fire burns away wickedness and serious illness. On that day, each family eats special food. Fried beans are eaten in the belief that they promote honesty. The women of the Bai Ethnic Group carry out a purification ceremony on snakes and insects in the corners of their houses. On the farms the process is repeated by torchlight, with the purpose of celebrating in advance an abundant harvest and a healthy community. The Bai use torches to throw light upon the rice ears, in this way offering up prayers for the grain harvest.

The custom of using fire to expel wickedness is also to be found in the Torch Festival of the Achang Ethnic Group held on June 24 of the lunar calendar. Holding torches, the people walk around the house burning off things such as cobwebs hoping by so doing to expel wickedness and preserve the security of the community. All the villagers, holding torches gather on the village square and then wander around the village, the hillside and the farmland in order to eliminate insect pests and celebrate in advance the coming harvest.

It is a similar story with the Hani Ethnic Group. On the last night of the festival, every family holds a torch and illuminates all corners of the house hoping to expel all bad fortune and wickedness. They then bring the torches to the roadside near the village and set up a row of firecrackers. The firecrackers which are arranged facing southeast, also help to drive away evil spirits from the community.

The main activity involved in the Torch Festival of the Gelao Ethinic Group held on the 6th day of the 6th lunar month also involves the villagers holding torches and parading around the village, hoping by performing this ritual to drive out all ill fortune and disaster, and to ensure a large family, bountiful harvest and healthy livestock. Here the Torch Festival is referred to as "sweeping the village", because the Gelao believe the ritual helps to cleanse the village and the community.

The Torch Festival of the Naxi Ethnic Group is for them second only to the Spring Festival in terms of ceremony and importance. Indeed it is also known as the "Small Spring Festival". On the first day of the Torch Festival, the longest and best pine tree is chosen to make the torch. On the night of the 25th, red, yellow and white wild flowers are also picked and put in vases on the middle columns of the torch. The whole village sets up this enormous torch, right in the middle of the village and decorates it with red-tasseled corn and trays of sunflowers. Every family contributes three pine torches which when lit send dancing sparks flying into the air and driving out, the people hope, all bad fortune and evil spirits. The direction the sparks fly is also used as a method of divination, determining magically whether or not there will be a good harvest. At dusk, the torches are lit in front

AUGUST 1 INTERNATIONAL HORSE RACE FESTIVAL HELD IN LITANG OF SICHUAN IN 2006

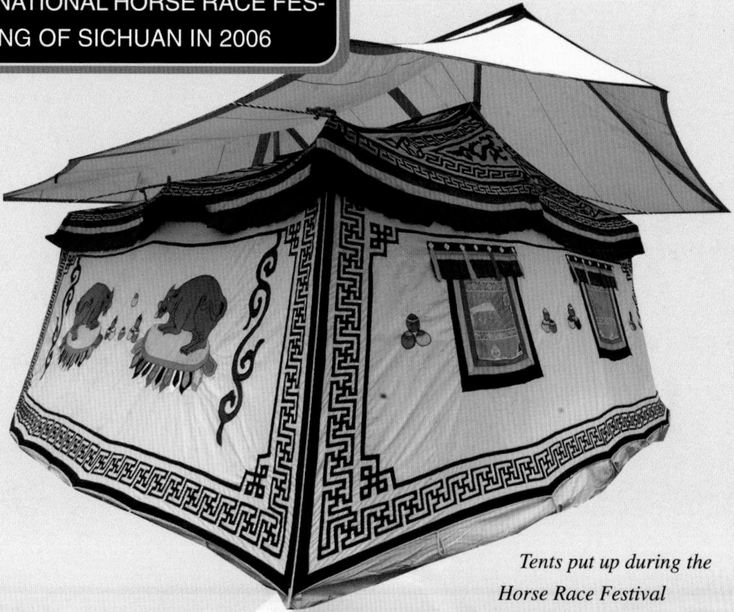

Tents put up during the Horse Race Festival

A shot of the Horse Race Festival

FESTIVALS

MONGOLIAN NADAM FAIR

Sacrificial altar on the grasslands

Mongolian wrestler

Mongolian herders practicing wrestling

Wrestling traditional to the Mongolians

Traditional horsemanship

TIBETAN SHOTON (SOUR MILK) DRINKING FESTIVAL

Giant portrait of Buddha unfolded

TIBETAN SHOTON (SOUR MILK) DRINKING FESTIVAL

Horse race held during the Shoton Festival in Tibet

Performance given in front of the Potala Palace

Lamas burning incenses during the Shoton Festival

Tibetan opera performance in front of the Potala Palace

FESTIVALS

BUTTER SCULPTURE AND LANTERN FESTIVAL

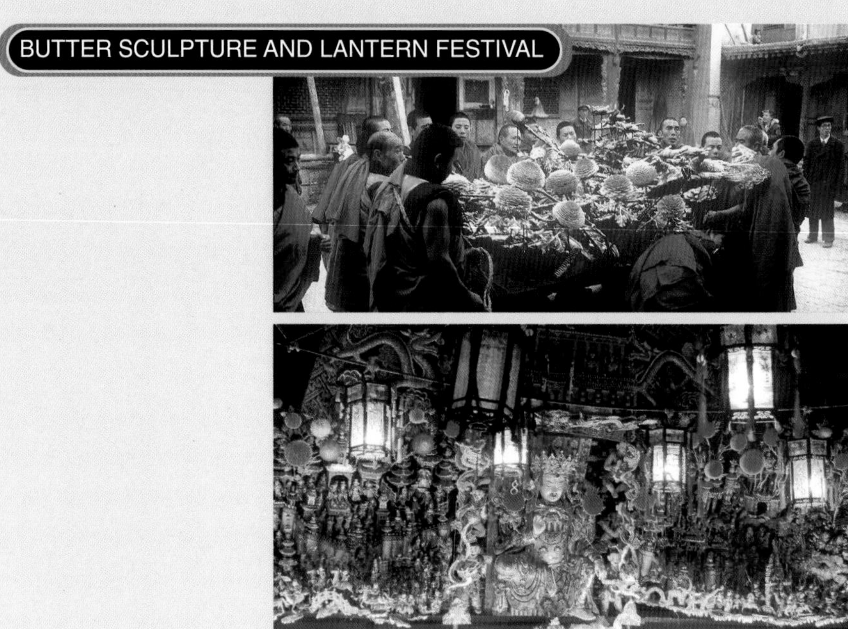

Butter sculpture and lantern festival held in the Tar Monastery of Qinghai

ONGKOR (BUMPER HARVEST) FESTIVAL OF THE TIBETAN RACE

Villagers attending the Ongkor Festival walk along the asphalted road

TIBETAN NEW YEAR

Holy dance performed in monasteries on the Tibetan New Year

On the Tibetan New Year, auspicious qingke barley is much favored as gifts

Tibetans put on their holiday's best

FAST-BREAKING FESTIVAL

Food used during the Fast-breaking Festival

Muslims in Ningxia celebrating the Fast-breaking Festival

CORBAN FESTIVAL

Iman of the Kashi Atidor Mosq

AKEN PLAYING AND SINGING PARTY OF THE KAZAK ETHNIC GROUP

TORCH FESTIVAL

FLOWER MOUNTAIN FESTIVAL OF THE YI

FASHION SHOW OF THE YI

Fashion festival of the Yi in Yongren County in Yunnan

Fashion festival of the Yi in Chuxiong of Yunnan

SHUAGETANG FESTIVAL OF THE YAO ETHNIC GROUP IN LIANNAN

of every family's door, and holding small torches, the people illuminate and send the smoke darting into all corners of their property——from the yard, to where the livestock is held, to the front gate and beyond, all the while muttering chants to help expel bad wind, rain, hailstones and illness.

The torch must be built higher day by day, and on the third day, the climax of the torch festival, the torch is hung with beautiful decorations. All four corners must be set ablaze in order to illuminate the crops, destroy pests and celebrate in advance a bountiful harvest. At night the people hold the torches aloft, singing and dancing all through the night.

Opinions vary as to the origins of the Torch Festival. The Torch Festival as celebrated by the Yi Ethnic Group during the period of Guangxu (1875-1908) is recorded in the *Kunming County Annals*. It is said these rituals were carried out to pay respects to a brave, clever and tender lady. It is also recorded in the Chuxiong County Annals as the Xinghui Festival. The Yi also believe that one needs fire to do battle with the demon, Siriyapi in heaven: a battle symbolically represented by the burning of insect pests to protect the crops. Activities held during the Torch Festival also include patrolling, wrestling and bullfighting. Yi legends record that in ancient times, the god, Entiguci often sent an emissary, Chekoshoff to collect taxes. However this agent always took advantage of the situation to cheat and cruelly oppress the Yi people. One day, he went to the family of Snorbargo to collect grain. He wanted a meal and wine and seeing that Snorbargo was not in, flew into a rage and threatened to kill Snorbargo. However, by chance he ate two mouthful of rice, which had been mixed with gold and silver and three of his teeth dropped out. Realizing that Snorbargo was more powerful than him, he fled to the forest in a panic.

Snorbargo later caught up with him and killed him after finding him cowering in a hollowed out tree. The god Entiguci was enraged by this and sent a plague of insects to eat crops in the world of man. Seeing this, one of the Yi leaders Yunque was quite sorrowful and sought to arrange mediation with the vengeful god. The people tried to collect together enough money to appease his wrath but eventually they were still nine liang of silver and nine qian of gold short. Just when the people were beginning to despair, Snorbargo thought of the idea of using heavenly fire. He instructed the people to light up torches, which they used to burn the insects. Thus they managed to ensure a good harvest.

This is why the people believe that the fire of the torch can drive out all the ghosts and evils from homes, villages and fields and ensure a good harvest In the daytime, they kill cattle and pigs to honor the gods and some also sacrifice chickens to pay respects to the father of the field and the mother of the land. Here, the torch has more than a purely symbolic meaning: it is used to purify the village of insects and to herald the coming

harvest. During the Torch Festival, each village also holds various social and cultural activities, including singing, dancing, horse racing, bullfighting, wrestling, archery, tug of war, and swing.

The legend related to the Torch Festival as celebrated by the Bai Ethnic Group also stresses the importance of paying respects to the ancient tribal heroes. One legend of the Ma Bai Ethnic Group (a branch of the Bai Ethnic Group) is that the gods punish human beings who have done evil by burning their villages. The elders however saved the day, preempting the wrathful god by asking the people to light up torches and thus rescue the whole village from destruction. A similar Naxi legend substitutes the Jade Emperor of Heaven for the gods.

As for the origin of the festival, the Gelao Ehnic Group have their own particular explanation which comes from their legends. They say that in ancient times their ancestors had fashioned for themselves a wonderful life but one god resented seeing people living and working in peace and contentment, so he sent a powerful demon to fight with the Gelao people. The brave people were undaunted and overwhelmed the demon. The god remained resentful, and transformed incense into a plague of insects which he sent to destroy the crops. However the resourceful Gelao ancestors picked up pine branches and dry bamboo and fashioned them into effective torches, which they used to destroy all the insects. In order to commemorate the victory and celebrate the bountiful harvest, the offspring passed on the custom of the Torch Festival.

Two legends of the Lahu Ethnic Group also seek to explain the origins of this festival. One tells of how on the mountain inhabited by the Lahu lived two supernatural creatures —— one a helpful, friendly entity, the other a malign destructive force. The latter delighted in devouring the eyes of the people, while the former always did whatever it could to help the people. Once, the good demon set pairs of horns made of beeswax on the head of hornless sheep. At night, the horns were lit up and the sheep ran on the mountain like numerous torches, so the evil demon became frightened and ran off leaving the people in peace.

Another legend tells how the cruel God Esha asked people to offer sacrifice to him every year. The brave and wise Lahu hero Chanochabi led the people in resistance to this order, which infuriated the god, who made the sun, moon and stars dim in the sky. Because of the dark, the people could not till the land. Chanochabi asked the people to use pine torches and beeswax fastened on the horn of cattle to illuminate the fields, and the crop were successfully tended. To commemorate the great Chanochabi, the Torch Festival is held every year.

In a broader sense one can see the ultimate origin of Torch Festivals in the worship of fire so common to primitive society, Torch Festivals in various areas of the Yungui Plateau are typically held at the time when the paddies have to be planted and the insects are at their most destructive. Burning torches and patroling the paddy field is a practical measure to help destroy insect pests and ensure a good harvest.

III. Tasting the New Produce Festival: Common to Many Ethnic Groups

Many ethnic groups in southern China, such as the Miao, Tong, Hani, Jingpo, Lahu are principally engaged in rice production. They typically hold festivals when the rice grows ripe and the harvest approaches. For example, the Tasting the New Produce Festival of the Naxi, and the Miao Ethnic Groups and the New Rice Festival, and Double Six Festival of the Bouyei and Tong Ethnic Groups.

The Kochacha Festival of the Hani Ethnic Group

The Hani people of Yunnan Province celebrate a festival which they call Kochacha. In the Hani Language, this word refers to the time when the crop is about to ripen and the abundance of harvest time is imminent. Held on June 24 of the Chinese lunar calendar every year, it lasts for between two and five days.

During the festival, the people prepare abundant food, and then kill domestic animals to offer sacrifices to the gods, thinking that the abundance of the harvest is dependent upon the protection of the gods. It is said that in ancient times, the Hani people worshipped a god named "Weizui", who would regularly come to the village in order to safeguard the safety of the people, ensure the health of the domestic animals and the abundance of the harvest. In order to thank "Weizui", the people held a grand ceremony to welcome the god as he entered their village and to expel evils and disasters and bless the people and pray for peace and happiness. This tradition passed down from generation to generation, and has become the festival as it is still celebrated today.

One of the most important activities of the festival is playing Moqiu,. This involves selecting a hard piece of wood between one and two meters long with a diameter of about 15 cm. The wood is fixed upright on the ground with another piece of wood 6 meters long placed horizontally on the top. When properly arranged you have a sort of rotating machine which can be used as a swing. When playing the game, the number of persons on the two

ends should be equal, and the people sit on the horizontal wood and rotate with it. Those on the side falling to the ground kick off from the ground with their feet and the other side goes down in turn. This can be quite a skilful exercise and many people crowd around the Moqiu ground to watch. The boldest young men hope with their superb Moqiu skills to win the admiration of the village girls. Besides this sport, the festival also features such activities as dancing, playing swing and wrestling. At night, all the villagers sit around the bonfire to listen to the old men telling ancient stories.

The Fresh Produce Festival of the Tong Ethnic Group

The Tong people, who have made a major contribution to the culture of Chinese rice cultivation, celebrate the Fresh Produce Festival. The festival is held in different areas at different times, Most hold it on the 6th day of the 6th lunar month of the lunar calendar, some on the first day of "Mao"(the forth earthly branch) after the small heat (a Chinese solar term) in June of the lunar calendar. Some select a different auspicious day each year and some insist on July 1 as the proper time for these festivities.

During the festival the people in the Liping area of Guizhou Province pick up between five and seven buds of standing grain from the field in the early morning, putting each a fresh grain of rice-bud on each bowl of food and wine. They then pay their respects to the ancestors by burning joss sticks and papers, and only after this ritual do they begin to eat. Besides chicken and duck meat, the food of the festival is characterized by sour flavored food. There is a popular saying which states that "the Tong cannot be separated from their sour food ". The sour soup fish is the special food of the festival, so on the day before the festival, every family goes out to catch fish in order to make the ten jins of dry sour soup fish that each household sees as necessary for the coming festivities. The sourness of the soup comes from the pickled and preserved vegetables that are used for ingredients and also from the water used to wash the rice and the liquid used in preserving the sticky rice in jars. The soup is extremely tasty and refreshing The pickled sour fish, braized or fried sticky rice, sweet wine, peppers mixed with Chinese prickly ash and salt can be preserved for decades.

The Fresh Produce Festival on the 6th day of the 6th lunar month celebrated in Huitong in Hunan Province is similar to that of Liping. They also pick several buds of rice from the paddy field. They then place three in their shrine, beseeching their revered ancestors to taste first, The remaining buds are pounded and crushed and cooked. This is the first rice of the year and is sampled by all family members one by one according to the position in the family hierarchy. When inviting the elders to taste first, they intone beautiful blessings such as "Bountiful harvest and healthy animals".

The Yuping Fresh Produce Festival in Guizhou Province differs a little from the above-mentioned areas. Every family picks some rice grains, kaoliang and corn, brings them back home and boils them, After honoring their ancestors with the cooked rice, 12 dishes are prepared from various meats and food, 12 wine cups are filled and 12 bowls laid out together. After a ritual of reverence for ancestors, everyone eats the new produce and gives thanks for the bounty of the harvest.

The festival as celebrated in Xinhuang in Hunan Province also has its own unique characteristics. It is said in Xinhuang that the festival is to commemorate ancestors such as Wu Shiwan who was responsible for first making of the barren land a fertile place fit for cultivation. The theme of the festival is to welcome the rice harvest and beg the blessing of the ancestors. The grand activity of "Gan'ao" is held that day in the areas of Xinzhai, and Mozhai. This is a social activity where men and women of the Tong community wear grand clothes, and listen to displays of antiphonal singing: musical dialogues between two persons with two voice parts. Favorites include the song of first-meeting, the song of praise and the song of borrowing. The people join in and make new friends, none more so than the young men and women who make use of the dialogue form of the songs to express their amorous emotions. The young man sing the "shang'ao" song, and invite their favorite girl to sing her response. In the past, the song of asking-surname is sung first because if the girl has the same surname and family branch as the man, they are not allowed to fall in love with each other and the song ceases immediately,. If no such barriers block the path of love however, the song continues and the lilting strains of lovelorn voices ring through the warm air.

The 6th day of the 6th lunar month Celebrations of the Bouyei Ethnic Group

In the old days, the 6th day of the 6th lunar month is for the Bouyei Ethnic Group the date on which memorial ceremonies are held and prayers are offered for a good harvest.

The Bouyei mainly live in Guizhou Province, distributed around different areas in which the 6th day of the 6th lunar month is called a variety of names: the areas of Pingtang and Huishui call it the Emperor Festival; those of Longli and Guiding call it the Insect King Festival; those of Wangmo and Ceheng call it the Dragon King Festival; those of Changshun and Huishui call it the Chengge Festival; those of Suyun call it the Catching June or June Bridge Festival.

The 6th day of the 6th lunar month is a special festival when the people hold various activities, which mainly fall into two categories. The first involves sacrificial activities.

Many villages hold ceremonies known as "Sweeping the farmland". On that day, every family makes a large number of small burgees using white paper, each pierced with a thin bamboo stick about two chi long. These burgees are placed at the edges of each piece of farmland. Then every household slaughters a pig in order to honor the deity of the village, the god of corn, and the god of land. They also hope this sacrifice may appease or even drive out the demon of drought, the ghost of flood and the locust monster thus ensuring a good harvest and preserving the wellbeing of the community. The area of Pan County is characterized by the worship of green seedlings, while in Wangmo County sacrifice is offered to the father of the field and the mother of the land. The Dragon King is also worshipped, in the hope that his protection may be bestowed on the people. The second category of activity involves playing on the mountain and singing, but nowadays this tradition has been transformed into large-scale song contests.

The Fresh Produce Festival of Jino Ethnic Group

A Fresh Produce Festival is also celebrated by the Jino people, but differs markedly from that of the Tong and Bouyei Ethnic Groups, in that it preserves a lot of ancient traditions passed down through history and legend.

The festival is held on the day dedicated to the Tiger (one of the twelve animals representing the twelve Earthly Branches) during August according to the lunar calendar when the rice is beginning to ripen. Firstly the elders of the village pay reverence to the soul of the paddy because their belief is that everything has a soul. Why shouldn't something as productive and as vital to the community as the paddy not have a soul? The people believe that only if the soul of the paddy is worshiped can the rice harvest be guaranteed. In some villages, the family who reap the biggest harvest hold the ceremony first. They pick a few ears of plump-grained millet and bring them back home where they are crushed and cooked. The way the rice cooks is said to be a portent of the next year's harvest: if the steam rises eastward, the family's children will thrive; if it rises westward, the hunting will be good in the coming year; if to the south, an abundant harvest will be reaped; and finally if northward, it bodes ill for all. After the fortune is told, each family offers the sacrifice of some new rice and a cooked chicken to the soul of the paddy and to the ghosts of their ancestors. The person offering the sacrifice sings some short three-character-line-poems to pray for the longevity of the people and an abundant harvest in the coming year. On that day, every household invites the elders and relatives to eat with them to taste the new food. The next day, the send a container of new rice and a piece of chicken to the ones who couldn't make it the day before. This festival today is very much one that celebrates the harvest.

The Ongkor Festival of the Tibetan Ethnic Group

The ethnic groups of Yunnan and Guizhou Province celebrate the rice harvest, but the people of Tibet celebrate the qingke barley harvest. When the crops ripen, they celebrate what they call the Ongkor Festival ("Ongkor" in Tibetan means "walking around the farmland".) The festival is held in August of the Tibetan calendar, the time when the people of the plateau welcome the harvest.

According to the record of *The Calendar Arithmetic of the Bon Religion*, as early as the fifth or sixth century, the farmers of the Southern Mountain began the practice of plowing using a furrow. Because of the geographic location of this region, sitting atop a great plateau, there is always the danger of wind and sandstorms, frost, snow and hail. In order to guarantee a good harvest, the elder of the Ben Religion leads the people in a parade around the village lands to offer prayers for the harvest. Chanting sutras all the while the elder holds the "Dada" (a wooden stick wrapped in Hada) and a gigot in front of him, as he is followed by the villagers, holding censers, and carrying grains of qingke barley and ears of millet. After the parade, they place the millet in the barn or shrine. In order to pray for a good harvest, the people also hold various activities, such as wrestling, sword contests and shuttlecock. The competitions are typically energetic and intense and the people crowd around to watch the action which is invariably followed by joyous singing and dancing.

According to scholarly research, the Ongkor Festival traces its origins back to an ancient agricultural tribe, who worshipped the land. It is recorded in the *Totem Volume of Tibetan Ethnic Group* that the totem most often revered in Tibet is the Twelve Danma Goddess. This goddess has varying and unique characteristics, some areas seeing her as a white Jokul God without flesh and blood; some regarding it as the empress of the Eagle King, flying on a white ribbon in the sky.

The Gelu Sect of Tibetan Buddhism in the 14th century inherited this traditional festival, and their Buddhist beliefs greatly influenced the celebrations. When patrolling the farmland, they hold aloft a statue of the Buddha, reading aloud holy sutras. Such practices continue to this day.

The Ongkor Festival is one of the most important Tibetan festivals. Wearing festive costumes, the people raise a 'harvest tower' full of millet, celebrating and singing happily all the while. Horse races, archery competitions and Tibetan Drama performances are also enormously enjoyed by one and all.

IV. Festivals Celebrating the Harvest

Heralding, praying for and celebrating a good harvest are concepts that go to the very heart and soul of traditional Chinese society, and unsurprisingly they are usually marked by important festivals. China is a large agricultural country. Even during the Xia Dynasty (roughly from the 22nd century BC to the beginning of the 17th century BC), sacrificial ceremonies to celebrate a good harvest were held. The nomadic peoples of the northern grasslands also have since ancient times held great festivals to celebrate the abundance of the earth and the bounty of a good harvest.

The Nadun Festival of the Tu Ethnic Group in Qinghai Province

The Nadun Festival is a traditional festival celebrated by the Tu people living in the Guanting, Zhongchuan, and Gangou areas of Minhe County, Qinghai Province.

"Nadun" means a time of play or a fair. The Nadun Festival, also known as the Harvest Festival, is a holiday when people celebrate a good harvest, and is in effect somewhat of a folk carnival of the Tu. The scale of the festivities very much depends on the size of that year's harvest. If the harvest is good, the festival is celebrated with enormous ceremony and elaboration. However when natural disasters result in a bad harvest the celebrations will be muted or will not take place at all. Nadun is celebrated collectively by the village, regardless of family allegiance. But very often dominant surnames will be prefixed to the festival giving titles like the Ma Family Nadun, the Song Family Nadun etc. Also the date when the festival is held varies from area to area. Generally, it depends on when the crops ripen. Generally speaking, Nadun is celebrated between the middle of July and the middle of September. Crops ripen quicker on the plain than in the mountains so the festivals tend to be held earlier in those areas. After the wheat has been harvested in late summer, the festival lasts for nearly two months until autumn. So it's also known as "the longest carnival in the world".

The venue where the Nadun festivities take place is set up with sedan-chairs and tents for the comfortable transport and lodgings for the God Erlang and the Dragon King. Besides three divine sedan-chairs set up by the villagers in the divine tent, other sacrificial offerings are made and gongs and drums are set aside for dancing that evening. Before the tent stands an eight-meter-high divine pole which is used to worship the heavenly and earthly gods. The tent and pole stand opposite to each other quite far apart, and constitute the two important poles of the festival venue.

On the day before Nadun, villagers fry dough cakes and make a special type of sacrificial cake known as Supan (literally 'crisp plate'). Bearing live sheep and chickens the people come to the divine tent to pray and present their Supan and hexagonal hangings decorated with token money and grain, expressing their gratitude to the gods for the bountiful harvest.

The Nadun celebrations take on many forms. It may be held by only one village or by two jointly, the latter form being most common, one village acting as the host, and the other the guest. In long lines, men from the two villages shoulder colorful banners, beat gongs and drums and congregate on one of the host's wheatfields. Then dozens of drums are beaten, the deafening and powerful drumbeats marking the official opening of the Nadun Festival.

The first activity is the Huishou Dance, a large-scale dance involving forty to fifty people who take part in sequence according to seniority. At the front dance the old men in long gown with fans in their hands, who usually are the organizers of the Nadun festivities. Next are found the young men with multi-colored banners that are inscribed with prayers like "Favorable weather" or "Celebrating a good harvest", and then come the children holding willow braches. They dance around the field while the hosts toast the dancers with big bowls, the whole scene being one of great merriment and fun.

After the dances are completed, the dancers kowtow and burn joss sticks before the divine sedan-chairs. At the same time the elders of the village offer eulogies to celebrate the good harvest and pray for next year's good weather. Then the clash and crash of gongs and fireworks echo through the air. And the dancers shout "hurray" and retreat to "battle array" formations. These arrays are a wonderful sight to see.

With a great joyous shout the dances begin. First up comes the chanting of good news and the beating of thick sticks. As a matter of fact, chanting the good news is a way of both opening the gate of heaven, opening the gate of the gods, and of inviting the gods in at last to the fair to celebrate the good harvest and a peaceful society. Beating the thick sticks provides the accompaniment to the dance performances offered up to the honored gods.

A performance is also given of the Nuo Opera (mask dance), including Zhuangjiaqi, Sanjiangwu, Wujiangwu. In Zhuangjiaqi (peasants), four people take the roles of father, mother, son and daughter-in-law. The father is a hard-working farmer, but the son is reluctant to till land. Worried, the father invites the old men of the village to persuade his son and the son finally comes around to his father's point of view. At last he inscribes the character "田" (field) with a plow, showing that farming and the continuity of farming

from generation to generation is a matter of fundamental importance to the life of the community.

The third aspect of the celebrations is the dancing of "Fala", which is a representation of inviting gods down to the earth to make merry with man. At last, the Supan offered to the gods is divided into big pieces and distributed among the villagers, to represent the bonds between man and god.

The Nadun Festival has been in existence since at least the period when the ancestors of the Tu people engaged in nomadic animal husbandry, which can be seen in the traditional dance "The Brave General Who Killed a Tiger". With modern developments in agricultural production however there has been a gradual shift from nomadic life to settling down in a place and embarking upon farming, and corresponding new dances have been produced reflecting this kind of life and mode of production.

The Mongolian Nadam Fair

On the vast grasslands in the north of China, there is a festival celebrated by the herdsmen to celebrate a good harvest. This festival is called the Mongolian Nadam Fair.

"Nadam" means "joy" or "game" in the Mongolian language. The festival falls around the time when spring becomes summer. The Nadam Fair is not held every year; it depends on the condition of the pasture and the livestock: it's held when the grass is abundant and the livestock are fat; in times of want it is not held. In the past, at least one Nadam Fair would be held every two or three years.

The period from May to July and August is the most charming season on the grassland, when water and grass are plentiful, livestock grow stout and strong, and the fragrance of cheese can be detected everywhere. Autumn on the grassland has intoxicated many sons and daughters; numerous tents are set up and herdsmen ride to the Nadam Fair from all directions. Pedlers from far and near also congregate to sell their wares. In olden times, sacrificial ceremonies would be held during this period: Lamas would light lanterns, chant scriptures and pray to the Buddha to ask that prosperity be bestowed on the people and ill-fortune be banished from the grassland.

The Nadam Fair is usually held at the same time as ceremonies worshiping Aobao. The Mongolians take Aobao as their patron saint. Worshipping Aobao is a way of showing respect to the heavenly and earthly gods, praying for rain and favorable weather from heaven; for plentiful grass, abundant grain and prosperous livestock from earth, and for peace and harmony for the community as a whole.

As the Aobao rites are observed, a meter-high sacrificial altar will be set up, on which are placed the heads of freshly-slaughtered cattle and sheep by prestigious Lamas. As wreathing smoke from joss sticks and candles color the air, herdsmen scatter wine and candies on the representation of Aobao; some also placing Lumafeng Banners made of colored paper around Aobao, before making three circles clockwise around the holy figure. After that, some kowtow; some attach white and blue Hada to the highest point of the icon-the divine tree branches just like arms beckoning the herdsman. Aobao-worship is a manifestation of Shamanism, reflecting the imperatives of the nomadic grassland existence.

After respect has been paid to Aobao, the Nadam Fair begins. This is a time when herdsmen can show their manliness. There are mainly three forms of athletic competition: horse-racing, wrestling and archery.

The Mongolians are practically raised on horseback and they hold special affection for horses. Horse racing can be traced back to the Han period, and has always been for Mongolians the ultimate test of manliness. During the Nadam Fair, it is the horse-racing competition that displays most clearly the courage and wisdom of the Mongolian people.

In accordance with nomadic existence, a bow and arrow is an absolute necessity. Not only Mongolian men but also women are skilled at archery. There is a wide range of contenders who take part in the contests, men and women, young and old. The pattern of the bow and the arrow, the range of the bow, the length, weight and range of the arrow, all depend on the individual and the ethnic group and region he or she belongs to. Archery on horseback is a magnificent sight. Archers of valiant and heroic bearing in festive costumes gallop about darting here and there like fish in water. They wield their bows, and shoot arrows effortlessly while galloping on horseback.

Wrestling rivals horse racing and archery as a popular activity among the Mongolian people. Wrestling is not only a test of strength but also a contest of wisdom and technique. Generally speaking, no age or body weight limits are imposed; nor are there any set rules as such. At the beginning, the two parties crouch facing each other, each grasping their opponent's waistband. It makes for a wonderful scene. A circle is set up on the field, in which sand is spread. Participators are divided into an east group and a west group. From each group, one or more wrestlers enter the arena, dancing in order to impress on their opponents their lion-like bravery. The winners are the ones who manage to throw their opponents to the ground. There are several skillful dancers and singers in each group. Whenever each individual contest comes to a climax, they will shout and sing in loud voices to inspire the wrestlers. But no matter what the result turns out to be, the wrestlers and the audience are united in joyous celebration of a shared culture.

FESTIVALS

On the field, other merry activities are held, such as Bulu throwing, horse lassoing, camel racing and so on. After the intense competition, the sweet sounds of the Matou Qin are to be heard; and the herdsmen abandon themselves to singing and dancing right through the night.

Harvest Sacrificial Rites among the Ami People of Taiwan

The Ami people of Taiwan are one of the clans of the Gaoshan ethnic group. Their Harvest Sacrificial Rites are held during the eighth month of the lunar calendar every three years and last 6 days. The participants in the first stage are exclusively females from the age of 8 to 28. It is widely believed that paddy fields are female and thus respond favorably to the women and bring forth a good harvest. Sacrifices include pigs, cattle etc.

The first day of this festival is the pestling day, when maids go to their lovers' home to pestle rice, which is called Kaisuodu. The second day is the god-worship day, when important ceremonies are held. The third and the fourth day are dancing days; at that time, maidens will give arecas to their dancing boyfriends as tokens of their love; elders of the tribes will award prizes to the three most industrious young men; the fifth day is also a dancing day, but only females dance while men look on; boys should present arecas to their girlfriends or kin; and young men should go to the seaside to catch fish. The sixth day is a communal fishing day; the young people who will part in the adult ceremony go to catch fish for the elders; and from this day these young people will live and serve in the chamber of the tribe for six years, during which they will not be allowed to get married.

As females are the representations of fertility, all the celebrants are females, symbolizing the celebration of, and the expectations for, a good harvest. The adult ceremony is also held at the time when the rice ripens, and thus celebrates the maturing of both man and crop.

CHAPTER III SACRIFICIAL AND COMMEMORATIVE FESTIVALS

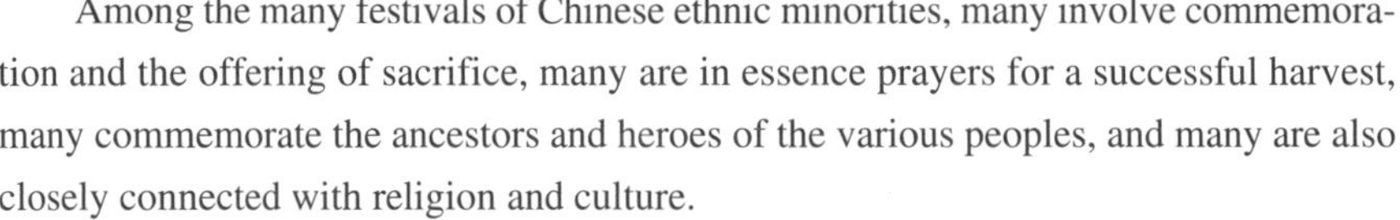

Among the many festivals of Chinese ethnic minorities, many involve commemoration and the offering of sacrifice, many are in essence prayers for a successful harvest, many commemorate the ancestors and heroes of the various peoples, and many are also closely connected with religion and culture.

I.Pure Brightness Day

Pure Brightness Day is the date on which sacrifice are offered to the ancestors. The people visit and sweep the tombs and recall the lives of their forefathers, a tradition going back to the Tang Dynasty (618-907). The ancestors worshiped on Pure Brightness Day include lineal relatives, the ancestors of one's own family and the heroes of the common ethnic group, as well as the common ancestors of China such as the Yellow Emperor, the Yan Emperor and so on. There are two ways in which respect is paid to ancestors on Pure Brightness Day: one is to worship the ancestors in the house or ancestral temple, called joined worship; the other is to visit a grave and sweep the tomb, called tomb worship The latter involves two activities: burning incense and offering up sacrifices to the dead; and repairing the tombs and erecting steles to commemorate decedents. The civilians believe that the campo santo is the world of the dead and the tomb is their house. Because of scouring rain and the trampling of wild and domestic animals, the tombs are always damaged, so they need to be repaired. No matter if one worships in an ancestral temple or visits a grave, burning incense and offering sacrifice are essential. When offering sacrifices, the Chinese always burn paper, which can be used in the nether world as money. The people sweeping the tomb also carry meat, wine and fruits and respectfully place them on the graves of the relatives where they are divided up and eaten.

Many of the Chinese ethnic minorities such as the Yi, Zhuang, Bouyei, Manchu, Tong, Yao, Bai, Tujia, Li, Lisu, She, Shui, Naxi, Mulao, Qiang, Maonan, Gelao, Xibe, Pumi, Russia, Ewenki, Jing, and Hezhe also celebrate Pure Brightness Days, and carry out rituals of ancestor worship during this festival.

The people of the Maonan ethnic minority have three ways in which their ancestors' graves are tended on Pure Brightness Day: each family offers sacrifices to the ancestral tombs separately; the brothers of an extended family together go to sweep their ancestor's grave; or the people of the united clan go together to worship the ancestors. When sweeping the grave, they have the custom of dining together on the campo santo. There are various kinds of food, and besides the common pork, beef, chicken and duck, a small piglet is slaughtered on the campo santo its lifeblood pouring out on the tomb as an offering to the ancestors. People eat "Matixiang" and like to eat the food by wrapping the cooked sour vegetables and meat in clean lettuce —— feast with a most distinctive flavor.

In contrast to the Han who place the paper money on top of the tomb, the Manchu people put willow branches on the grave when they visit to honor their ancestors, believing the willow to be a human forebear. In order to show that the family line continues, the willow branches are placed on the tomb. Chickens are also sacrificed and good wine offered up. After the rituals of worship, the wine, rice and other dishes are placed beside the grave while repairs are carried out.

The Li people do not usually sweep graves on Pure Brightness Day after offering sacrifices but in many cases nowadays the follow the Han practice. The Zhuang have the custom of washing bones for the dead who have died recently. The washed bones are then "buried for the second time".

The Lahu and Achang peoples of Yunnan Province also worship ancestors on Pure Brightness Day. At that time, every household prepares wine and rice and sweeps the graves of their own family's ancestors, erecting steles or moving the grave——whatever is necessary. According to Lahu customs, before sweeping the grave, it should be leveled up with extra soil, the weeds should be cleared away, and only then can the wine, meat, rice and other dishes be placed on the grave to honor the dead. Some small animals are then slaughtered and offered as sacrifice. After the ceremony, all the people sit around together and have a picnic, sharing out the food between them. However, the Achang people in the early morning of Pure Brightness Day, first renovate and repair the graves. They then place willow branches around the grave, and crush a kind of wild edible yellow flowers to make "the yellow flower Baba of Pure Brightness Day", with which, they prepare wine and dishes. On returning back after visiting the graves, they offer sacrifice to their ancestors in the temple hall. On the day, important families slaughter pigs and cattle for a feast.

Taqing (going for a walk in the country in spring) is another important activity popular at this time of year. Since ancient times, it has been a custom for people to stroll about at this time taking in the enchanting scenes of spring. After the worshiping ceremony is finished, the tomb-sweepers always sit down to rest, but many prefer to go traveling and visit places of interest. In many places Pure Brightness Day is also called the "Taqing Festival", which became most popular during the Tang Dynasty. Du Fu's poem Pure Brightness reads:

"Prosperity exists here and there today,
Thousands of people come out in Changsha.
The green willows along the river are bright and gorgeous,
But the horses crowding on the road are so impatient
They gnaw each other's knees."

The Picture of Bian River On the Pure brightness Day by Zhang Zheduan, a North Song Dynasty (960-1127) artist, depicts a scene of people returning home after sweeping tombs and going for a spring walk in the countryside. When strolling in the countryside,

activities such as willow shooting, push-and-pull, playing ball, catching butterflies, picking up grass, flying kites, cockfighting and playing swing were also held.

There are many types of food associated with Pure Brightness Day, most being related to religious beliefs. For example, the famous "Zhengmianyan", also called "Ziduiyan", is painstakingly prepared by the womenfolk in order to commemorate Jie Zidui. Every family in the Lin'an area of Zhejiang Province gathers tender lotus root and mixes it with sticky rice to make "Qingminggou". Both Zhengmianyan" and "Qingminggou" are foods thought to have symbolic and actual power. It is believed they can help to expel evil and also get rid of illness and provide valuable nutrition to the body. Spring Cake is another kind of important food associated with Pure Brightness Day. Originally used to worship the ancestors, this cake later became a common food. In addition, malt dust and cold porridge are also commonly consumed at this time. When discussing the food customs of Pure Brightness Day, "Wuren Rice" of the She Ethnic Group must be mentioned. Eastern Fujian is the heartland of the She people, and on March 3 every year, each She family cooks "Wuren Rice" and sends some to Han relatives and friends.

Gradually, the local Han have also acquired the custom of eating "Wuren Rice". "Wuren Rice" is not difficult to prepare: first, one cleans the leaves of Wuren trees and then puts them in boiled water; second, one takes out the leaves and immerses the sticky rice in the Wuren soup for nine hours; finally, sticky rice is boiled and is ready to eat. Though the cooked "Wuren Rice" is black in color and looks most unappetizing, the wonderful fragrance of the rice soon reaches one's nostrils and you feel a great desire to taste the unique flavor of this fascinating food. The people of Kurong County offer "Wuren Rice" as a sacrifice every year, and it has become a She custom passed down from generation to generation. Because the She and Han have intermarried, having "Wuren Rice" has gradually became a common dietary custom of both groups in Eastern Fujian Province.

II. The Dragon Boat Festival

The Dragon Boat Festival, a time-honored traditional Chinese festival which falls on the fifth day of the fifth lunar month, is one of the best known of all Chinese festivals. The Dragon Boat Festival has been celebrated by Chinese people for over 2,000 years.

This festival is known by a variety of other names, such as Duanyang, Chongwu, Wuyuewu, Puwu, Pujie, Tianzhong Festival, and Poet's Festival. It is celebrated by as many as 26 ethnic groups, including the Han, Manchu, Korean, Daur, Tu, Tujia, Bai, Hani, Dai, Lahu, Naxi, Zhuang, Bouyei, and Li.

It is generally believed that this festival is related in some way to Qu Yuan (c.340-278 BC), a patriotic minister of the Chu State during the Warring States Period (475-220 BC). He advocated elevating to positions of authority men of virtue, thus enriching the state and building up its military power. Qu Yuan advocated forming an alliance with the Qi State in order to resist the powerful Qin State but this policy met with intense opposition from many of the Chu nobility, most notably Zi Lan. These nobles spread rumors and blackened Qu Yuan's name and eventually the minister was forced to retire from office. Ultimately he was even driven out of the city and sent into exile in a remote valley near the Yuan and the Xiang River. In exile, he composed many wonderful heart-rending poems such as Lisao (The Sorrow of Separation), Tianwen (Heavenly Questions) and Jiuge (Nine Songs). This is perhaps why this festival is also known as the Poet's Festival. In 278 BC, the capital of the Chu State was overrun by its enemies. On hearing of this fateful attack upon his motherland, Qu Yuan was heartbroken. Everything meaningful in his life had been taken away and destroyed. On the fifth day of the fifth month, just after finishing his last poem Huaisha he threw himself into the Niluojiang River carrying a heavy stone in his arms to ensure he sank to the bottom. Various folk-customs sprang up in memory of Qu Yuan on what came to be known as the Dragon Boat Festival.

Another explanation of the origin of this festival concerns Cao Er. Cao Er, a dutiful daughter, was born during the Eastern Han Dynasty in Shangyu. Tragically her father was drowned in a river and for several days his body wasn't found. Cao Er, at the age of fourteen, went to search for her father's corpse by the grassy banks of the river. She leaped into the water and after an exhausting couple of days searching through the cold dark waters, she finally succeeded in finding her dear father's body.

Many also believe that the fifth month is an important time in terms of agricultural production especially silkworm spinning and therefore on this day they worship the God of Agriculture and the Silkworm God.

Zhang Tianshi and Zhong Kui are both Taoist historical figures. Some Chinese peoples believe the fifth month to be the "Evil Month" and the fifth day of the fifth month to be the "Evil Day". Zhang and Zhong are deities believed to have the power to drive out evil spirits, so naturally people on this day offered sacrifice to them.

The various ethnic minorities have their own unique legends about the festival.

The legend explaining the origin of the festival in Banqiao Village, Qiaohou Town, Eryuan County, Yunnan Province goes like this: long ago the crops and livestock of the village were plundered, and the womenfolk raped by an evil warlord named Shagula. One brave couple, who loved each other very much, dared to resist. The hero fought against Shagula on the fifth day of the fifth lunar month. After a bloody and terrible battle he

perished together with the enemy. Later, people saw a pair of eagles flying west. They were believed to be the embodiment of the great hero and his loyal consort, their eternal love taking new shape. From then on, every fifth day of the fifth month, the Yi people celebrate this day with community activities such as horse racing on the great plain.

Many ethnic minority legends associated with the Duanwu Festival deal with love; many also involve resisting oppression and protecting one's homeland, but a common feature is paying respects and homage to a prominent hero from within their own ethnic group. According to the Dai people, especially those who live in Wuwanhe Ba, Yuanyang County, Yunnan Province, a pair of lovestruck young people drowned themselves in the Laobing Dalong Pool because their parents objected to their marriage. In memory of the tragic couple, people gathered under the mangoes of the Dalong Pool to spend the Zongzi Festival (another name of the Duanwu or Dragon Boat Festival). Meanwhile for the Zhuang people of Ning County, Guangxi Province, this festival is an occasion on which sacrifice is offered to the Water Goddess Baimuniang. Two lines of the popular lyric, *The Duanwu Sacrificial* Song reads:

"Rowing our boat to go to pay respects to Baimuniang;
The sound of fireworks echoes across the sky."

The Lahus plant trees and bamboos. It's said this day is the time when the corn seeds begin to germinate, and it is also believed to be the best time for planting new trees. The Lahu also prepare wine and meat for their guests and relatives to celebrate the occasion.

The fifth day of the fifth lunar month is called E'Ri'E'Zu by the Qiang people. On this day, men stay at home to mind the house while the women go out to offer sacrifice on the mountains,. The womenfolk sing haunting songs and perform elegant dances (they call them Shalang) for the enjoyment of each Qiang household in the village.

III. Other Commemorative Festivals on which Sacrifices are Offered

Since respect and reverence for one's ancestors is common to every ethnic group, the day on which respects are paid to these ancestors has for many ethnic groups become an important festival.

Danu Festival

The Danu Festival is the largest memorial festival of the Yao Ethnic Group in the

Bama, Du'an, and Nandan areas of Guangxi Province. Danu in the Yao Language means, "Don't forget", and the festival is also called by some the Zhuzhu Festival, the Zuniang Festival, the Yao New Year or even the Two-nine Festival. The timing of the festival is not fixed: some celebrate it once a year, some every three or five years and some only every twelve years. Beginning around the end of May by the Chinese lunar calendar, the Danu Festival in most Yao areas lasts for three to five days.

The Danu Festival of the Yao Ethnic Group is said to commemorate an ancestral goddess called Miluotuo, who was believed to have created the world and mankind. After creating the moon, the sun, clouds, and all living things, she began to fashion human beings using beeswax. The first batch of humans were ten men and ten women, called Buqing and these became the Han Ethnic Group; the second were nine men and nine women, called Buqiang. These became the Zhuang Ethnic Group; the third were eight men and eight women, called Bumiao. Thus began the Miao Ethnic Group. The fifth batch were five men and five women, called Bunu who would eventually produce the Yao people. Some time later, all the people of Han, Zhuang and Miao got up early one morning to explore the confines of their world. The Yao people slept late that morning and thus were the only ones present when Miluotuo delivered an important lecture on how best to open up the wasteland and cultivate the soil, how best to fell trees to build houses, how best to hunt animals for food, how best to beat drums to drive away pests and predators and how best to ensure a good harvest each year.

The other legend goes like this: Miluotuo gave birth to three children and after they grew up, she asked them to make their own way in the world. The eldest one held a weighing scales and engaged in business, setting up a family whose offspring would constitute the Han Ethnic Group today; the second carried a furrow and began to plow the land settling down, to become the Zhuang Ethnic Group today; but the mother gave the youngest a selection of small grains. He climbed the mountain and tried to cultivate the barren land. However, the wild pigs and mice wrought terrible destruction on the crops and after one year's backbreaking toil, the third child had nothing, not even the seeds he began with. His mother offered valuable counsel, advising him that, "there is a copper drum in the house. If you carry it with you, it can help you drive away the birds and beasts and bring you happiness". The youngest son followed his mother's advice: whenever the wild animals approached, he began to beat the drum, so the ferocious animals dared not come close enough to damage the crops.

Once when she had grown old and weary, Miluotuo found the youngest son and told him, "May 29 is your mother's birthday, so you should bring your wife and offspring to come to honor me, so you can have ample food and clothing and live a happy life." After returning home, the son boiled rice wine, killed chicken and ducks, steamed sticky rice and then brought his children dressed in their finest clothes to congratulate his mother on the occasion of her

birthday. Because this mother goddess is called "Danu" in the Yao language, meaning "Don't forget", the Yao Ethnic Group holds a grand festival this day to commemorate her.

The Danu Festival is also held in the Du'an, Dahua, and Bama Autonomous Counties of the Yao Ethnic Group in Guangxi Province and Donglan, Pingguo, and Mashan Counties of the Zhuang Ethnic Group in Bunuyao mountainous areas, from May 26 to May 29. From May 26, every family worships their ancestors, preparing a jug of rice wine and offering it to Miluotuo along with other sacrifices. In the stillness of the night, housewives quietly wrap glutinous rice dumplings, calling the unsuspecting family to eat only after the food is cooked. On the 27, the old men organize cockfights; on the 28, the people kill pigs and sheep, and prepare a great feast for relatives and close friends, all the time beating copper drums and singing toasting songs; on the 29, all the men and women of the village get together to carry the meat and wine and drums up to the top of the mountain, singing all the way. The men and women sing antiphonal songs and bang their copper drums. The middle-aged men and elders drink wine and make jokes together and the children let off firecrackers and learn to beat the drums. Activities such as horse racing and archery are also organized. In some areas, so-called Copper Drum Dances and Hsinglangticho Dances are held as people let off enormous firecrackers, play with spinning tops, sing songs and drink wine. This is the climax of the Danu Festival, which takes place on May 29.

Panwang Festival of Yao Ethnic Group

Pan Wang is the great ancestor of the Yao Ethnic Group, and is celebrated in festivals such as "Dancing Panwang", "Making Panwang", "Returning the Wishes of Pan Wang" among others in the areas of Guangxi, Hunan, Guangdong, and Yunnan Provinces. The festivals take place in different areas at different times, but they are usually held sometime during the slack season in autumn. The Yao Ethnic Groups in Northern Guilin, Hunan and Northern Guangdong Provinces mostly hold it between the middle October by the Chinese Lunar Calendar to the Spring Festival. In August 1984, Yao Ethnic Group representatives in various areas got together in Nanning, Guangxi Province, and arrived at an agreement that from then on, on October 16 by the Chinese lunar calendar the Panwang Festival would be celebrated.

This ancient festival commonly lasts for three days and two nights, but some communities celebrate it for as long as seven days and seven nights. It can be celebrated by individual families, as well as by clans made up of a number of families together or whole communities. The festival consists of many fascinating and colorful activities: for example, dancing the tambourine dance, and singing the Panwang Song, historical songs, love songs and harvest songs. In some areas the people also play the flower stick, set off elaborate firecrackers and enjoy the singing of theatrical troupes. As a notable traditional ethnic dance, the Panwang Dance is an indispensable part of the festivities. This is an elaborate dance which includes more than ten movements including "Beginning the dance" and "Calling on the Dragon". The dance can last for anything from one to two days, and is accompanied by the cheerful sounds of the tambourine. The dancers writhe, rotate and jump in a series of wild gestures, performing actions representing the opening up of the wasteland, the planting of trees, chopping wood and planting seeds. Meanwhile all the girls circle around the action, singing beautiful Panwang Songs.

The original religious element associated with the Panwang Festival as celebrated by the Yao relates to totem worship and ancestor worship, Nowadays such practices have evolved into the splendid festivities as celebrated today, commemorating their ancestors and giving thanks for the harvest.

The Sword Pole Festival of the Lisu Ethnic Group

One festival which focuses not on commemorating common ancestors, but rather on remembering local tribal heroes who have made a major contribution to the development of the ethnic group, is the Sword Pole Festival.

Popular in the Bijiang, Fugong, and Lushui areas of the Nujiang River populated by the Lisu Ethnic Group in Yunnan Province, the Sword Pole Festival is held on February 8 by the Chinese lunar calendar every year. The festival is said to have begun during the Ming Dynasty (1368-1644). During the reign of the Ming emperor Zhengtong, a tribal leader named Luchuan Tusi colluded with foreign forces to invade the border area of Yunnan, in a vain attempt to threaten the territorial unity of the empire. The Ming Minister for War, Wangji received orders to march against Luchuna, The main fighting force would be made up of Lisu men. Lisu generals and soldiers suffered the most severe hardships and fought the enemies bravely, and succeeded in driving out the invader. Though Wangji was of the Han race, he helped the Lisu people defend their homes and inspired them to continue cultivating their crops, protect their forests, and feed their domestic animals while the young men of Lisu took up the sword, training day and night, to fight the enemy.

As often happened in imperial China though, the valiant commander Wangji, was a victim of jealous court intrigue and the foolish emperor, believing the slanders, recalled him to Beijing and treacherously poisoned him to death during a dinner of welcome on February 8 by the Chinese lunar calendar. In order to commemorate Wangji's patriotic defence of the frontier forever, the Lisu people held activities every year, a custom which has passed down from generation to generation and gradually evolved into the Sword Pole festival as celebrated today.

During the festival, the people wear special costumes and gather from far and near for the festivities.

The "Jumping into the sea of flames" contest is held first. This hair-raising competition involves setting bucketfuls of firewood alight on the ground where five strong young men jump into the flaming buckets bare-footed. Sometimes they even jump on the fire and roll in it, fearlessly leaping up with the glowing ball of fire in their hands, wiping it on their face several times. By this purification-by-fire ritual, the community believes that it will be saved from various disasters in the New Year.

On the second day, the "Climbing up the mountain of swords" contest is held. In the middle of the contest area are placed two large 20-meter long, thick bamboo poles. Often 36 or even sometimes 72 long swords are inserted in the pole with the blade upward. This is called the "sword pole". The climbers are always strong young men and receive long-term training to master the art of climbing the pole. Before the climbing begins sacrifices are offered: a number of bare-footed warriors, dressed from head to toe in red, walk fearlessly to the pole where they go down on their knees in front of Minister Wang's picture, holding their hands over their heads and chanting respectful prayers. They then take one drink of wine. After some singing and dancing around the poles, the men suddenly jump on the first sword of the pole. Up they climb oblivious to the razor sharp steps of this curious "ladder". When they get to the top, they perform extremely difficult actions such as standing upside down. They then set off firecrackers in celebration. The audience cheer excitedly and compete for the honor of being allowed to offer the finest wine to the sword-climbing heroes. All wish to pay their respects to these fearless warriors.

The activities of " Climbing up the mountain of swords" and "Jumping into the sea of flames " include activities such as counting flowers, counting swords, playing swords, welcoming flowers, setting up the sacrificial altar, worshiping the sword pole, erecting the pole, offering sacrifices to the dragon, putting on the swords, taking the swords off, jumping into the sea of flames and so on. All rituals must be carried out according to strict customs.

As the Lisu people see it, the ritual of "jumping into the sea of flames" drives out evil and infection and prevents flood and fire. "Climbing up the mountains of swords" is a rite of passage for the men of the village, demonstrating their strength and invulnerability.

After the two activities are finished, the young men and women hold activities such as dropping cigarette cases, antiphonal dancing, and playing swing, all of which add enormous interest and color to the festival.

CHAPTER IV RELIGIOUS FESTIVALS

Throughout China's long history numerous folk religious practices have become popular among various ethnic minorities. Many of these religious beliefs and customs date back to the remote past and penetrated the popular consciousness to such a degree that they have evolved into colorful festivals. Established world religions like Buddhism and Islam became very popular in China and, as all religions invariably do, they assimilated many of the old folk customs, giving many of these festivals their unique flavor.

I. Folk Religious Festivals

Chinese ethnic folk religious belief is various and widespread. Since ancient times, they have formed an integral part of people's material and spiritual life.

The Munao Festival of the Jingpo Ethnic Group

Nature commonly served as the object of worship in most primitive religions. In these religious systems, heavenly gods were of enormous importance. Every ethnic group had the customs of worshipping heaven, a remnant of which also remains in folk sacrificial rites and festivals. The Munao Festival of the Dehong Jingpo-Dai Ethnic Group Autonomous Prefecture of Yunnan Province is just such a festival that developed from heavenly-god worship.

The Munao Festival is the Munao Zongge, which is a Jingpo phrase meaning "the crowd dances together". In the past, the Jingpo people worshipped the heavenly god Mudai, and the festival was the occasion on which they offered sacrifice to Mudai. It is the most important festival of the year for the Jingpo, and is celebrated within nine days of the 15th day of the first lunar month every year and lasts between three and five days.

During the festival, four 20-meter-high and 60-cm-wide wooden tablets known as the Munao Tablet or Stake will be erected. These tablets are carved with elegant patterns usually referring to one of the following themes:

- the Snow mountains-Muzhuaishenglabeng, the birthplace of the ancestors of the Jingpo people
- women's breasts: a representation that all Jingpo people derive from the same ancestor.
- the sun-the eternal source of light and heat, and all forms of life.
- the moon and the stars-the monarchs of the night sky, which can light the way for the Jingpo people when all other light fails.

● helical, gyral and ripple patterns-showing a long migratory road full of hardships and twists, which is also a representation of the dance steps performed during the Munao Zongge.

● divine broadswords and double-edged swords-representing the courage, valor, and enterprise of the Jingpo people, as well as their history of war, migration and struggle, and indeed of their using of swords to cut pathways through the mountains.

● Peacocks, hornbills, denoting that the Munao Zongge owes its origins in legend to these creatures.

● rhombic designs and the designs of brake tender leaves: the rhombic designs symbolize fruit, and in a wider sense plentiful food for the community

● five grains of cereal and six domesticated animals-expressing the Jingpo hope for abundant grain and healthy livestock.

Set before the Munao Stakes are two high platforms, from which it is said the Jingpo people can gaze at the Himalayas, where their ancestors used to live, and indeed gaze into the future. The stakes around the high platforms are decorated with eight gongs, drums and other musical instruments as tokens of good luck. All the stakes and platforms are enclosed by two circles of bamboo fences - a representation of victory. At the same time, divine stakes and platforms are usually set up around the field and livestock and fowl are slaughtered as sacrifices. Traditionally, people mainly offer sacrifice to Sanwa, the Blood God, Malizhitong, the Earth God, Wazi, the Water God, as well as the Gods of Mountain, Thunder and Wind during the Munao Zongge. If it is a collective Munao Zongge, the Tongsa (celebrant) of each stockaded village should hold a memorial ceremony for the Village God, while if it's held by just one family, they offer sacrifices to the Family Hall God and the Mudai God.

At this festival people mainly dance the Munao Dance. Two old people at that time wear peacock-feathered hats. In this way people keep in mind at all times the legendary origins of the Munao Festival. Following the two old people, other people begin to enter the field. Men hold long broadswords in their hand or carry Xiangjiao (elephant foot) Drums; all the time waving handkerchiefs, veils, ornate fans, and leaves, ladies will dress up in festival costumes decorated with dazzling silver pendants. When dancing, each man faces a lady, advancing towards and retreating from their partner. Songs are also sung in memory of their ancestors.

There are three legends concerning the origin of this festival dance. The first holds that the people learned this dance from birds, who brought it to them from the Sun God. The second teaches that long, long ago, the Jingpo people lived a happy life in a remote,

but beautiful place. But one day, a demon appeared in their midst and the people were plunged into hardship. A Jingpo man name Leipan led a revolt against the intruder and the demon was finally destroyed. People were so joyful at this deliverance that they sang and danced to celebrate the victory. The third story relates to Ningguanwu, who, the Jingpo people believe is their Creator. At his parents' insistence, Ningguanwa went to the Sun Realm to learn the Munao Dance. There, a dazzling peacock was acknowledged as the leader of the Munao Dance. It dictated all the steps of the dance and carefully directed everyone. After Ningguanwa's had learned the steps, he organized dancing parties in the human world. At the the foot of the Himalayas (said to the birthplace of the Jingpo people) he set up a dancing area, staking out this area with great wooden, carved stakes and demanding the leaders of the dance wear peacock-feathered hats in order to commemorate the generosity of the heavenly peacock who had taught him the dance.

Despite the differences between the three stories, they do share a general element of worshipping the sun and eliminating evil. By singing and dancing, people render their respect and prayers to the heavenly gods: "We worship and offer sacrifice to you; may you bless and preserve the health and peace of our village; may all disease and slander remain outside our gates and may the people lead a comfortable life free from cold and hunger."

The Ha Festival of the Jing

The gods worshiped by different ethnic groups vary according to ecological environment and mode of production. For the Jing people who live by fishing in Hainan Province, their beliefs are expressed during the Ha Festival. In their language, "Ha" or "Changha" means singing. But there is much more to this colorful festival than just singing.

A venue is set aside for celebrating the Ha Festival, namely the Ha Pavilion. The Ha Pavilion is a spacious building built with choice timber, not only firm but also beautiful. A memorial figure of the Sea-Deterring King stands in the main hall of the Ha Pavilion. The so-called Sea-Deterring King in fact is a human representation of the Sea God who keeps the people safe from the ravages of the ocean and also ensures the fishing harvest. In the pavilion there are also found other representations of gods and tablets of all the local family names. The tribal ancestors have been transformed into gods, so besides the sea god, the people there still pray to their ancestors to ask for their blessing. In this sense, the Ha Pavilion functions as both an ancestral temple and a shrine. Inside the hall, there are places for the Ha girls to dance and sing. On both sides are sets of three-tiered steps, which allows people to cross their legs and 'zuomeng'. 'Zuomeng' is the word the Jing use for the action of drinking while watching the dances and listening to the songs. People take their seats according to age and the amount of money they have donated. Only men over eighteen are entitled to sit down to 'zuomeng' while women and children have to stand outside to watch and listen.

Offering sacrifice to ancestors is an activity of the very first importance for the Jing during the festival. People prostrate themselves before the Sea-Deterring King, burn joss sticks, kowtow and then worship their ancestors with great reverence. In their eyes, both the king and their ancestors are closely connected to their everyday lives.

The songs of the Ha Festival are called Ha Ge (Ha songs). There are many songbooks in circulation, in which the lyrics are written as set down by the Jing people in the late 13th century in Chinese characters. The performances are held either in the Ha Pavilion or outside. The activities held inside the pavilion are formal and serious while outside things are much freer as young people sing love songs in antiphonal style. In the pavilion, "Ha ge" are only sung by certain people. Usually, there are three roles: the "Ha Older Brother", who plays the Qin, two "Ha Younger Sisters", who take turns acting as the main singer. At the beginning of the performance, the main singer stands in the center of the hall with two bamboo strips in her hands, singing. Meanwhile, the other girl sits to one side, playing the Bangzi (slit drum). At the same time, the "Ha Older Brother" accompanies on the Qin. The songs are harmonious and sweet-sounding; and the music of the Qin is refreshing and soft. "Ha ge" speaks eloquently of the life of the Jing people.

The Ha Festival is also a very important social occasion for young people: many boys and girls select their life companion via activities like singing antiphonal love songs.

During the course of the performances, traditional dances such as the Tiaotiandeng, Taioyue, Huagun Dances will be performed. Tiaotiandeng was formerly a religious dance. With plates holding burning candles on their head or in their hands, girls dance wildly along to powerful beats. Similarly, when performing the Tiaoyue, the dancers whirl more and more quickly as the beats get stronger. On the whole, it's a scene of enormous fun and energy. The Huagun ("floral stick") dance uses rotating floral sticks as its main movements. As the rhythm quickens, the movements quicken correspondingly.

In different places, this festival is celebrated at different times. For the two islands Wanwei and Wuxing, it falls on the 10th day of the 6th lunar month (nowadays in Wuxing, it has changed to the first day of the 8th month); for Shanxin Island it the 10th of the 8th month; for Hongkan Village, it is the 25th of the first month. Changha can last three for between seven days and nights. The songs and dances here are ultimately recreational activities performed to honor the gods. However, in some places, the festival also

functions as a send-off for the gods.

In relation to the origin of this festival, it's said that, around seven or eight hundreds years ago a supernatural being skilled in the art of song came to these areas to teach the Jing people singing and dancing as well as, first, one would imagine, organizing them to resist the oppression of feudal rulers. The immortal hero died in the revolt and the Ha Festival was then established in her memory. Many believe however that the cultural connotations of this festival go far deeper than this.

II. Buddhist Festivals

The forms of Buddhism most popular in China include Han Buddhism and Tibetan Buddhism. The Mongolian, Tibetan, and Tu Ethnic minorities are all predominantly Buddhist, but all have, over many centuries, evolved their own individual, unique Buddhist tenets and customs. The most striking expression of these vibrant religious cultures are the series of festivals celebrated throughout the year by the various peoples.

Ghee Flower Light Fair

Tibetan Buddhism boasts a number of famous festivals, including the Monlam Conference, held in a temple in Lhasa, from January 4 to 25 by the Tibetan calendar. The Freeing Captive Animals Festival is held on January 8 in Labrang Temple in Gansu Province, the Sunning Buddha's Portrait Festival is held from May 14 to 16, the Milarepa Persuading Law Conference is held on July 8 and the large-scale Dancing As Deities Festival is held on December 29 at the Potala Palace.

The Ghee Flower Light Fair, held on January 15 by the lunar calendar every year, is the busiest religious festival associated with the Prayer Meetings held in January in the Ta' er Temple of Lusha' er Town, Huangzhong County in Qinghai Province. It is a festival with a history of more than 400 years.

The shapes of the ghee light flowers are splendidly beautiful, containing the stories of the life of the Buddha and that of the Wencheng Princess. The wondrous shapes of the eight great Tibetan Dramas are also depicted. Landscapes of mountains and rivers, buildings and pavilions, plants and animals all in graceful disorder are also featured. Indeed every spectrum of life is represented, some figures as high as two meters have as many as two or three hundred characters inscribed within. On the other hand some are only a couple of centimeters high. All in all, it is a scene too beautiful for words.

On January 15 by the lunar calendar every year, the monks of the Ta'er Temple use flutes, suona horns and golden bells to play wonderful "Pergola Music", with various florid ghee flowers displayed on the flower shelf. People flock in great crowds to witness this great Buddhist scene.

Water-splashing Festivals

Buddhism is divided into Mahayana and Hinayana branches, which closely related. Mahayana is a sect, which separated from Hinduism during the first to second century AD. They advocated liberating all living beings from the mortal world, while Hinayana only believes sentient beings transcend the human world to reach Nirvana. The Dai Ethnic minority who are mainly Hinayana Buddhists, celebrate many festivals such as the Water-Splashing Festival and the Door-Closing and Door-Opening Festivals. The Door-Closing and Door-Opening Festivals are also celebrated by the Blang Ethnic minority who are also Hinayana Buddhists.

According to the Dai Calendar, the day when the sun enters into Taurus (when the Paddy Rain Festival celebrated on April 21 begins every year) is the Water-Splashing Festival, which usually lasts for three days. The first day is meant to send off the old year and the third to welcome in the New Year.

Dragon boat races are held on the first day of the Water-Splashing Festival. The competitors wrap red brocade around their heads and use special long oars. When the Mangluo Gong, one of the favorite music instruments of Dai Ethnic Group is sounded, the dragon boats race on the water towards the horizon. When the race finishes, the people beat Mangluo Gongs and Elephant Foot Drums to express their happiness.

On the second day of the festival the joyous Water-Splashing is held. Gourds of clean water are collected in basins and barrels, and people chase after each other eager to inflict mutual soaking. The splashing of water symbolizes blessing on, and a wish for happiness for, one's friends and neighbors. Some young men splash water on their favorite girls and take the opportunity to express their deep love for the girl. The people have a great time in the course of splashing the water, getting rid of defilement and praying for good luck.

The Water-Splashing Festival is also the grandest of the festivals of the De'ang Ethnic minority, who also adheres to the Hinayana Buddhist faith. It is held from April 14 to 16 by the solar calendar every year and lasts for three days. In the early morning on the day before the festival, all the people wear grand clothes. The girls especially make great efforts to dress themselves with dazzling beauty. The old men bring sacrifices such as prepared food, colorful long narrow flags, incense and wax strips and place them before

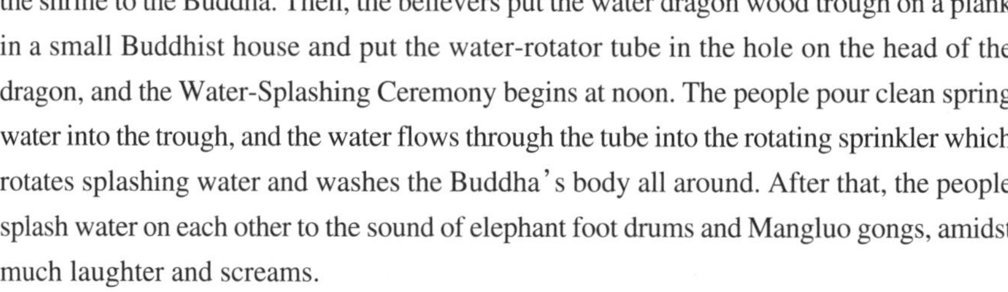

the shrine to the Buddha. Then, the believers put the water dragon wood trough on a plank in a small Buddhist house and put the water-rotator tube in the hole on the head of the dragon, and the Water-Splashing Ceremony begins at noon. The people pour clean spring water into the trough, and the water flows through the tube into the rotating sprinkler which rotates splashing water and washes the Buddha's body all around. After that, the people splash water on each other to the sound of elephant foot drums and Mangluo gongs, amidst much laughter and screams.

"Bai Ganduo"

The Buddhist festivals of the Dai also include "Bai Ganduo". From September 15 by the Dai Calendar every year, the Dai elders begin to "Enter into Wa", which means entering the Zang House (Temple) to worship Buddha. After three months, "Coming out of Wa" takes place, which is a ceremony to welcome the Buddha's return to the world. The second day afterwards is December 16 by the Dai Calendar, when the "Bai Ganduo" also begins.

The timing of the festival varies in different areas according to the number of large and important temples in the area. Generally a temple holds one "Bai", for between three and five days.

The venue for the festivities is commonly set up on a spacious square with huge green trees all around to offer natural cool shade. The people wear grand festival clothes and carry proudly the sacrifices they wish to offer, led by the music of the elephant foot drum band as they march to the ceremonial ground. They first go to the temple to burn incense and worship the Buddha, praying for offspring and wealth as well as peace. They then go to the festival market, where a vast smorgasbord of trinkets, food and items of interest are all arranged for sale. The stirring sound of the gongs and drums, the performing of peacock dances and Dai drama all make this a highlight of the year for the Dai people.

III. Islamic Festivals

After being introduced to China many centuries ago, the Islamic religion became assimilated and took on its own unique characteristics that make it today recognizable as the unique cultural expression that is Chinese Islamic culture. There are altogether 10 Islamic ethnic groups: the Hui, the Dongxiang, the Bonan, the Salar, the Uygur, the Ozbek, the Kazak, the Tajik, the Tatar and the Kirgiz. The people of these ethnic groups live together with Han people as well as with people of other ethnic minorities in a harmonious and neighborly fashion. However they are very careful to preserve their own religious beliefs, and observe their own particular festivals.

The Corban Festival

The Corban Festival is celebrated by all ten Islamic ethnic groups. It is called "Eid · Corban" or "Eid-ul-Adha" in Arabic. "Eid" means festival, while "Corban" and "Adha" mean "slaughtering and offering animals in sacrifice".

This festival owes its origins to the religious legends of ancient Arabia. It is believed that Ibrahim, the great ancestor of many Arabs in the north, had a dream in which Allah suggested he offer his son as a sacrifice to show the extent of his piety. At the very moment when Ibrahim with knife upheld was just about to kill his son as a sacrifice to God, Allah intervened, satisfied with the faith of Ibrahim, and ordered him to sacrifice a lamb instead. From this story has evolved the Islamic custom of slaughtering and offering domestic animals in sacrifice. After Islam was founded in the seventh century by Mohammed, this ceremony was adopted as part of Islamic practice; the Corban Festival also evolved into one of their most important religious festivals.

This festival falls on the 10th day of the 12th Islamic month. The Islamic calendar starts from the year when Mohammed moved from Mecca to Medina, the year known by the Chinese Islamic Hui people as "the First Year When the Sage Moved The Capital" (equates to 622 AD). According to the Islamic calendar, one year is divided into 12 months; every odd month has 30 days; and every even month consists of 29 days; there are neither leap months nor leap years. So every Islamic year is some 10 or 11 days shorter than a year according to the Gregorian calendar. Thus over three years, the Islamic calendar will fall one month behind the Gregorian Calendar. Therefore, if one goes by the Gregorian calendar, there is no set time for the Corban Festival.

During this festival, the Hui people, led by their imams, bow and kneel towards the west. During prayers, people recollect what mistakes or misdemeanors they have made in the past year, while the imam delivers the "Wartz", i.e. some teachings and other regulations, which need to be observed. At last, people say "Salaam-Alikoum" (meaning health and peace) to each other. Besides preparing food like zhayouxiang (fried round pancakes), sazi (oil fried wheaten food) and huili, the Hui people also slaughter cattle, sheep and camels. For economically comfortable families, each member should offer up a sheep in sacrifice; for less well off families, seven people together can slaughter a cow or a camel.

Many rules and regulations govern the slaughter of animals. For instance, lambs less than two years old and calves and camels less than three years old cannot be slaughtered; livestock that are blind, lame or without ear (s), or tail are also not allowed. They only choose healthy and strong beasts for sacrifice. The meat is divided into three portions: one part for themselves; one for their relatives; and one is given to charity.

Like other Moslems, the Uygur people also celebrate the Corban Festival on the 10th day of the 12th Islamic month every year. Before the festival, they clean up their homes and prepare various foods, like roasted nang, boursak, sazi, and krikqia. On the morning of the festival, people first bathe and put on fine clothes and then go to the mosque to pray and socialize. Afterwards they visit the graves of their families to pay their respects to the dead. When returning home, they slaughter sheep and cattle and prepare delicious dishes to entertain their guests and relatives. Usually, Moslems take the opportunity afforded by these festivals to pay calls on friends and relatives.

The Corban Festival as celebrated by the Kirgiz falls on the same day and lasts between three and fifteen days. Preparations for the festival begin from the time when lambs are delivered in the spring. The animals to be sacrificed are carefully selected. One of the black rams born each year is always slaughtered. On the eve of the festival, every family cleans their house and prepares pastries, fried sazi, roasted nang, and gets their new clothes ready. On the day of the festival, people bathe, dress up and go to worship in mosques. When they get back home, they slaughter some animals, the meat being boiled and cooked and used to entertain guests. They then visit relatives and friends. During the festival, activities like sheep snatching, horse racing and wrestling are also held.

The Tajik people living in Xinjiang also celebrate the Corban Festival. They regard this festival in the same way as other ethnic groups as regards such aspects as the legend of origin, time, worship and the performance of sacrifices. The differences lie in the fact that they spend this festival on the basis of their own traditional customs, and their material and spiritual life. They begin the preparations for this year's festival the previous year. During the period when lambs are born, every family picks out a lamb with dark eyes and pure white wool, which will be used for the next year's sacrifice. At the time of the festival, the lamb's eyes are beautifully painted and it is carried up to the roof and slaughtered. The blood of the lamb will be daubed on the children's foreheads and cheeks for luck. The lamb should be wholly boiled and sent intact to the people of Chama'atihana (the Tajik mosque). After worshiping, all the people gather around a table and enjoy the mutton distributed by the community as a whole, while reminiscing about the things that have happened during the year and look forward to the future. When the meal and prayers are finished, the people

MIAO SYSTERS FESTIVAL

Preparing colorful glutinous rice

Miao girls in the rape flower fields

FESTIVALS

PANWANG FESTIVAL OF THE YAO

Nuo Opera (mask dance) performance

Paying sacrifices to Panwang

DRAGON BOAT FESTIVAL

Object used to dispel the evils in Gansu

Miao girl ready to sing during the Dragon Boat Festival in Guizhou

Men of the Miao involved in the dragon boat race

WATER-SPRINKLING OF THE DAI

Wow!

Dragon boast race

A SCENE OF THE HINAYANA FESTIVAL OF THE DAI

THE MUNAO FESTIVAL OF THE JINGPO

Men holding long knives celebrate the festival

Jingpo men wearing masks sing and dance

Munao Zhuang

Tujia boys and girls sing to express what is in their mind

A Canadian bride groom during the wedding

French woman recording the Hand Wielding Dance of the Tujia

FESTIVALS

PURE BRIGHTNESS FESTIVAL

Paying sacrifices to the Yellow Emperor at Huangling County of Shaanxi during the Pure Brightness Festival

Sharing "tomb cakes" during the Pure Brightness Festival is a custom of Zhejiang

Tomb sweeping is a custom of the Tujia

DANCING FLOWERS OF THE MIAO

The Flower Dancing Festival begins with paying sacrifices to the flowers tree

Merry Miao dancing is very entertaining

Miao people cross mountains for the Flowers Dancing party

NADUN FESTIVAL OF THE TU

GELAO PEOPLE AT THE TASTING THINGS FRESH FESTIVAL

Gelao girls praying for a better life

Paying sacrifices to the ancestors

Gelao youths gathering things fresh

CLIMBING KNIFE LADDER FESTIVAL OF THE LISU

Site of the Climbing Knife Ladder Festival

"Jumping Over Fire"

Standing the knife ladder

Feet not hurt at all

Lisu girls during a festival

PARTYING SINGING OF THE DONG

FLOWERS PARTY

FESTIVE CELEBRATION OF THE HANI

Performing drum dance to pay sacrifice to the autumn

Solar drum dance

DANCE OF THE JINO

Celebrating the bumper harvest

1,000 people involved in the dance

Bronze drum dance

Merry Boyi people

FESTIVALS

SINGING FESTIVAL OF THE BOYI

Bamboo Tube Dance of the Boyi

Boyi people demonstrating singing skills

Watching performances in the teeth of scorching sun

Bamboo hats available at festive market

NEW YEAR CELEBRATION OF THE DULONG

THE RAO SANLING CELEBRATIONS OF THE BAI IN DALI, YUNNAN

Happy villagers

SIYUEBA FESTIVAL OF THE MIAO

MIZHI FESTIVAL OF THE YI

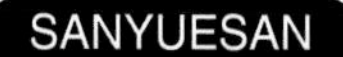

On the Sanyuesan Festival, She people sing in bamboo groves

Miao play lusheng to celebrate Sanyuesan

Bamboo Pole Dance of the Li on the Sanyuesan Festival

Li elders perform how to get fire by screwing wood in Hannan on the Sanyuesan Festival

TIGER FESTIVAL OF THE YI

GRAND MIAO NEW YEAR FAIR

travel in groups to pay visits on friends and relatives and offer holiday greetings.

The Eid or Fast-Breaking Festival

The Festival of Fast-breaking is another very important festival for the ethnic groups who believe in Islam. This festival, also called "Rozah", together with the Corban Festival and the birthday of the Prophet constitute the three biggest festivals in the Islamic calendar.

According to the teachings of Islam, Hui and other ethnic Chinese Muslims fast for one full month during Ramadan (the 9th month). Like all Muslims during Ramadan they fast from sun up until the crescent moon appears in the night sky. The fasting lasts until the evening of the 29th day; if a crescent moon appears at that time, people are free to break their fast the next day but if not, the fast continues for another day and the Festival of Fast-breaking falls on the second day. During Ramadan, Muslims neither chant nor eat: nor even the swallowing of saliva is permitted. Only after the sun sets can they eat and drink. Sexual intercourse is also forbidden during the fasting period. Overall this abstinence is seen as something that can help to improve one's character. If someone should die during this period, it's regarded as the best time at which such an event should take place.

The day after the end of Ramadan marks the beginning of the Festival of Fast-Breaking. Muslim men should firstly bathe and go to the mosque to pray and listen to the imam's sermon. Then they join in the festival activities.

The customs of the festival are different in different places. On this day, people of the same clan will go to cemeteries to pay their respects to their dead relatives or friends. People will greet each other in the traditional Islamic way, saying "Salaam-Alikoum" whenever they meet on the road or at the door. Relatives and neighbors also prepare rich food and set out all kinds of fruit in order to entertain guests who come to visit. The imam is invited to read the scriptures and preach, and a number of other entertainment activities are also organized.

There are many old tales and legends connected with this festival. One story tells of how in the remote past, the Islamic people fled to a desolate and uninhabited mountainside to escape the invasion of brutal foreign invaders. They dared not light fires in the daytime for fear that the enemy would discover them. When the moon rose at night, they would light a fire and cook some food. For generations, this practice endured; and finally it evolved into a custom. In the past, people only ate at nighttime during Ramadan. However, nowadays in these modern times, some families have forsaken the custom of fasting in the daytime believing it could damage their health.

The Night of Bailati

The Hui people living in the northwestern part of China celebrate Bailati Night on the 15th day of the 8th Hui month, which they also call "Zhuang Night" or "Nian Night". "Bailati" is the transliteration of a Persian word that means confession. It was said that Allah would decide the various destinies of humankind on this night. Another story holds that on this day Allah descends to the lowest part of Jannah (Heaven) and absolves the dying from their sins, making it easier for them to enter Paradise. So on this day, most Hui people fast during the day, worshipping, giving alms and praying to Allah for his blessing. In olden times, people would invite the local imam to read the "Bailati" from door to door of the community. This would signal the end of the festival activities.

The Birthday of the Prophet

The Birthday of the Prophet is one of the three greatest Islamic festivals. It is said that Mohammed (who lived between about AD 570-632), the originator of Islam, was born and died on the same day of the year: namely, the 12th day of the 3rd Islamic month. Therefore the followers of Islam assemble on this day to commemorate him. Afterwards, this day evolved into an important festival.

Muslims attach great importance to this festival, the activities of which are celebrated in mosques. At this time, they dress in their best clothes and bathe in the mosque. They then change clothes, worship, listen to the imam's sermons and reminisce on the life of the Prophet Mohammed and his wondrous teachings. These formalities completed, the people rest or perhaps take a pleasant stroll.

CHAPTER V RECREATIONAL FESTIVALS

At purely recreational festivals, people take great delight in socializing with their relatives and friends; in singing and dancing and having a good time. Various competitions and entertainments play a prominent role in these types of festivals, a good example being traditional Chinese Festivals of Song.

I. The Horse-racing Festivals of Nomadic Ethnic Groups

Traditionally, the Mongolian, Kazak, Kirgiz and some Tibetan peoples led a nomadic existence, moving from one place to another seeking hunting prey or fresh pasture for their livestock. Horse riding thus became an integral part of the lives of theses nomads, both in terms of herding livestock and animals, and occasionally doing battle against other ethnic groups. Many festivals of horse-racing are celebrated by these "Horse-Riding Ethnic Groups", such as the Mongolian Nadam Fair, the Tibetan Ongkor (Bumper Harvest) Festival and Greater Prayer Ceremony (Mon-Lam-chen-po).

Horse-racing

Horse-racing can be divided into three categories: horse racing contests, horse walking contests, and steeplechases.

The horse racing contest usually takes place over general terrain designated as a racetrack, the length of which can be anything from 20 to 40 kilometers or more in length. The contest mainly tests the speed and endurance of horses. The one who reaches the end point first wins the race. At the beginning of the race, the sight of dozens of sleek horses galloping off under a blue sky like arrows shot from a heavenly bow is truly a spectacular never-to-be-forgotten scene.

The horse walking contests are somewhat different. Such events test the patience, the steadiness and the grace of horses as well as their speed. Here the horse must walk elegantly rather than gallop crazily. The horses which are used in these contests are adult horses over five years old; the riders are also strong and robust adults.

The steeplechase racecourse usually includes mountainsides and rugged mountain roads. The length is usually somewhere over five hundred meters. This type of contest is most common in Tibetan areas.

A great hero needs a swift horse; a swift horse needs a hero. In horse-racing, horse and man become one. To best display his wondrous horsemanship, the rider firstly must have a good eye for choosing a good and suitable horse. He must then train the horse and become familiar with its habits and characteristics. One month before the contest, the racer will "slim the horse", which involves warming up the horse by reducing its fat content and overall weight, in order to strengthen its endurance. Before the contest, the mane of the sleek and lean horse is tied up to keep it out of the horse's eyes and its tail trimmed to reduce wind resistance. Some riders fasten colored ribbons to the horse's mane and tail. The multicolored ribbons serve to easily distinguish the different horses. The riders will also give the horses a thorough washing, and tie on bronze bells, necklaces as well as colorful ribbons to their manes. In this way, the horses present a beautiful sight to the watching spectators during the various competitions.

The riders' costumes are also elaborately prepared. They must be both light and soft. The light material minimizes the weight the horse must carry and a soft material easily absorbs sweat. The robes the riders wear are short, and close-fitting to reduce wind resistance. The riding boots worn are soft, supple and light. Being chosen to compete as a rider in the horse-racing contests is a great honor. The riders dress in gay costumes:, the front, cuffs, sleeves, and trouser legs of which are embroidered with elegant patterns.

Large-scale horse racing is held during the Nadam Fair. Sometimes small-scale horse races will also be held by herdsmen at ordinary, non-festival times.

Horsemanship

In addition to horse-racing, the nomadic ethnic groups also are very skilled at performing various other activities and tricks on horseback, demonstrating their unrivalled horsemanship. Some of the most prominent of these activities and tricks are listed below:

Polo: Polo is a game very popular among herdsmen. The field of play is set up on the vast grassland. On one side of the field stand two pillars around which a net is hung constituting one set of goals. The polo ball is as big as a fist. The players are divided into two teams. On horseback, they use a long club, shaped at the end into a crescent. The two teams then contend for the only ball seeking to drive it into the net and score a 'goal'. The team who scores the most "goals" will win. The competition is very intense and exciting. On the field, the skillful riders, sticks in hand, charge and check, changing direction effortlessly, leaning over to whack the ball and driving their mounts forward in pursuit. Historical chronicles show this to be an ancient sport, played for many centuries. It has had a variety of names and today is still extremely popular among the Tajiks.

Sheep-snatching: The Hazak, Kirgiz and Tajik Peoples of Xinjiang all love the game of sheep snatching. Usually, there are two ways in which this contest is organized. The first involves a sheep being laid on the ground. The contestants then gallop their horses ahead, striving to be the first to snatch the sheep. The one who not only snatches the sheep first but also takes it to a certain spot is the winner. The other method involves using a headless sheep carcass with hooves removed as a sort of game 'ball'. One of the contestants begins the game in possession of the sheep carcass and the other riders throng around in an attempt to forcibly grab it from him. The game is one in the same way as the first version and the winner keeps the sheep carcass as a trophy. Contestants can compete as individuals or as part of a team. In order to get the sheep, the riders sometimes swarm together, sometimes gallop apart like meteors, sometimes hang upside down from their horses; all the while galloping at top speed. It truly is a most exhilarating spectacle.

There origins of sheep-snatching go back to the the heroic epic Manas of the Kirgiz people. It is said that when Manas was fighting against his enemies, he used a lamb in just this way to train his soldiers and improve their horsemanship the better to triumph over their enemies. The Hazak people regard sheep-snatching as a spiritual activity: a prayer for happiness. The winner places the lamb at a random door, and happiness and luck inevitably come to the lucky family.

Catching up with girls: The Kazak and Kirgiz peoples of Xinjiang also greatly enjoy horse-racing, which they name "catching up with girls" or "girls chasing after boys". At the beginning of the game, young boys and girls ride forward neck and neck to a certain spot, where the lad teases and expresses his love for the girl. While the girl gallops her horse away, the lad must chase after her. If he succeeds in catching up with her, he is entitled to propose to her. This is just the so-called "catching up with girls" of the Kirgiz. For the Kazaks, the game is known as "girls chasing after boys". In this game, girls ride behind boys. When the young lad gallops his horse away, the girl chases after him and tries to lash the boy with her whip. This is also, believe it or not, a way of expressing love.

Picking up things on horseback and hiding oneself under the horse's back :

Another marvelous sight is when the horse is in full gallop the riders bend low to pick up things from the ground; whoever is first to reach a set place wins. This game requires amazing horsemanship. The things on the ground can be stones, handkerchiefs, or silver coins; in some places they pluck red banners. The Kazak people pick up handkerchiefs and silver ingots while the Tibetans pick up hada. For the Kirgiz people, the objects are usually silver coins. Four or five coins are placed on the ground at five or ten meter intervals. Beside each coin stands a person with a whip. When the riders lean over to pick up the coins, the persons beside the coins whip the horses and the rider must retain control of his mount. When training soldiers, in ancient times the hero Manas used to lay down daggers on the ground which his cavalry officers had to try to pick up while riding at full speed. This rigorous training evolved into the sport as practiced today.

The horsemanship of Tibetan women is well known. One contemporary report states; "There are several-inch-high poles every 30 to 40 bu. The women on horseback drive their horses swiftly and lean over to pick up the poles. Whoever picks up most poles wins".

Hiding oneself under the horse's back means when riding the horse the rider puts one foot in the stirrup and with one hand grasping the mane or the saddle, he just bends his legs and leans over until he is pressed up against the abdomen of the horse. The horse is galloping and the rider is still in control. However all you can see is the horse: the rider is hidden. In the Qing Dynasty, contests of horsemanship were popular among all northern ethnic groups and formed the climax of major sports events.

The Horse-racing Fairs of the Tibetan Ethnic Groups

The Horse-racing Fair of Damxung County, Tibet, is held at the end of the 7th Tibetan month or the beginning of the 8th month every year and lasts between five and seven days. At that time, Tibetan peasants and herdsmen from hundreds of kilometers away come in their beautiful festive costumes, riding fine horses and driving carts, to participate in this great fair. On the vast grassland a village of white tents is erected. The smoke rises into the clear sky; the horses whinny and the people are happy. All become immersed in a festive mood.

The opening ceremony is very interesting. In front people carrying red flags lead the procession. They are followed by the tightly grouped horse riders. The horses are decorated colorfully and the riders wear beautiful clothes. When all pass by the platform, they salute and let out exultant shouts. Various feats of horsemanship are then held: some riders bend incredibly low to pick up hada, their horse's gallop never slowing; some pluck banners or slash flagpoles; some shoot arrows at targets while galloping; some perform other amazing feats of horsemanship; some gallop wildly to demonstrate the speed and endurance of their horses.

After these contests comes the yak racing. The yaks, decorated with colorful ribbons, run here and there as their masters shout instructions. It is a most amusing scene.

At the intervals during these activities, people browse in the market purchasing necessities or just checking out the various market stalls.

When the curtain of night finally falls, heaped bonfires are lit. People gather around, singing, dancing and drinking wine and tea with great joy and festivity. In the stillness of the cool night, young couples ride off to secret places of seclusion to be alone together.

II. The Singing Festivals of the Northern Ethnic Groups

Songs are an essential aspect of the cultural expression of many northern ethnic groups. They sing to show their aspirations. Of the singing festivals, the "Flowers Party" is the most important. Held on June 6 on Lotus Flower Mountain, this festival is celebrated by northwest ethnic groups including the Han, Hui, Dongxiang, Bonan and Salar. The other most important singing festival is the "Aken Playing and Singing Party" celebrated by the Kazak people.

Flowers Party

The Flower Party as celebrated by the Tu people on Five-peak Mountain in the Huzhu area of Qinghai Province, is held on June 6. This festival has a long lineage. There are three styles of singing: solo, antiphonal, and choral. The songs range in subject matter from astronomy to geography, history and legends to social life and of course love. The flower songs can also be divided be into two distinct types: " Linxia Flowers" and "Taomin Flowers".

There hua'er Festival or the are differing explanations as to the origin of the Flower Party in different areas and among different ethnic groups. In Danma in Huzhu Autonomous County in Qinghai Province the Tu people believe that Danma was originally a place blessed with abundant flowers, grassland and forest, and when June arrived, bringing with it a profusion of brilliantly-colored flowers, the local young people of the community would all gather to court and sing flowers songs. But one year a leader of the tribe, disapproving of this practice, chopped down all the trees in order to forbid the people to celebrate these festivities. After that, it didn't rain for some three years and famine set in bringing enormous suffering to the people. One year in June, a pair of young people sang sorrowfully the forbidden flower songs, and a deluge of rain began to fall from the heavens. The people went wild with joy and sang loudly. However, after the rain, the lovers were transformed into two leafy poplar trees, which now stood on the green. From that time forward, the people came to this place to sing every year.

Some Tu people believe that the origins of the festival can be traced back to five sisters. Long long ago, there were five beautiful Tu sisters with voices as clear as bells, sweet and harmonious. When they sang, birds flying overhead would be so enchanted that they would stop flapping their wings and fall to earth. The clouds in the sky would stop moving, the water of the river would come to a halt and buds would instantly bloom on the tree. Many young men came from far and near and for three days and nights they sang their own songs in reply but none had a voice to match any of these nightingale sisters. On the morning of the fourth day, five cotton white clouds carried away the five sisters. They became five " Flower Fairies". The festival of song is celebrated on June 6 of the lunar calendar every year to commemorate the five sweet-singing sisters.

During the Flower Party, the people of different ethnic groups from different villages gather at the venue for the festivities, usually sectioned off with rope on the slope of a hill. When you approach this entrance a question will be asked of you in song. Only if you can reply in the proper way are you allowed to pass. Groups of three to five young people sing antiphonal songs. Some lyrics are traditional, and some are impromptu: made up on the spot as one asks and the other answers questions in song. As night falls, the antiphonal song party continues, sometimes till dawn. This festival remains extremely popular today.

Aken Playing and Singing Party of the Kazak Ethnic Group

On the grassy plain on which the Kazak people live on China's border to the west, the festival where the aken is played and traditional songs are song is one of the most interesting of the ethnic festivals of song in China.

The most popular of the many styles of singing in the Aken Playing and Singing Party is the antiphonal style, which is almost like guessing a riddle. Energetic and humorous, it is a style very common among the people. To begin, one female singer sings a riddle in song with the antiphonal male singer answering in the same way. If he does not sing his reply fluently and humorously, the male singer will lose face and the audience will tut with disapproval. Another typical style of antiphonal song is usually used by young people as entertainment and games. The songs can also function as a means for young people to express their feelings of love —— this type of song, when humorously and well-performed can result in brilliant smiles and joyful laughter.

While this Aken playing and singing festival places great emphasis on antiphonal songs between two persons, some are also sung by four people. Sometimes, the singer plays the dongbula (a musical instrument) while singing antiphonally, and the lyrics as well as the music are improvised on the spot. During the festival, the people watch and listen to the singers attentively and discuss their relative merits. From the level of applause

and cheering that each respective singer gets it is easy to see who are their favorites.

III. The Singing Festivals of the Southern Ethnic Groups

Many ethnic groups living in the southwest areas of China celebrate festivals of song. Some of the most notable are the Gexu and Ganpo Festivals of Song held in the Dong villages near Zhuang Town, the Zoupo Festival of the Mulam Ethnic Group and the Lusheng Festival of the Miao Ethnic Group.

The Singing Festival of the Miao Ethnic Group

The Miao people are synonymous with their culture of song and singing and a number of festivals of song are held throughout the year. Among the Miao of the Tujia Autonomous County Ethnic Group in Luxi County, Western Hunan Province, almost all the people can sing well. When climbing the hillside slopes on the way to work, "mountain songs" are sung; when chopping firewood, there are the "chopping songs"; when dining with guests, there are the "toasting songs"; when seeing a visitor out, there are the "farewell songs"; when courting, there are the "love songs"; when getting married, there is the " Epithalamium", and in the olden times, the "Crying because a loved one is Getting Married Songs". Songs are an integral part of people' s everyday lives. They sing not only during festivals, but during almost every aspect of their everyday activities. The festivals though, which are usually held during the slack season after the harvest, are the ultimate expression of this link between people and song.

The most important festival of song of the Miao people in Luxi County is held on June 6 by the lunar calendar in a small market town of Liangjia Tan Township where Luxi, Jishou, Guzhang and Yuanling Counties meet. The festival is staged near a mountain stream on the top of a mountain. In the early morning, the young people gather, milling together and chatting excitedly on the mountain peak, near the brook. The festival attracts huge crowds of people. When the singers begin, the audience is immediately respectful and silent - the voices reverberate and echo across the mountain and laughter soon follows.

Perhaps more interesting is the smaller singing festival held on the slopes of the mountain by a stream or in a small wood. Here the emphasis is on freeform antiphonal or 'crossing' songs. As a female and male singer converse in song, the people sit around and listen attentively. As the tone changes, so too do the lyrics; wise questions are asked and smart, humorous answers are given immediately, with great imaginative and verbal skill. All things provide content for these improvised songs —— nature, philosophy, ideas, gossip. It is an amazing display.

The Chabai Song festival of the Bouyei Ethnic Group

The Chabai Song festival of the Bouyei Ethnic Group compares favorably with the Miao singing festivals in terms of interest. On June 21 by the lunar calendar every year, young Bouyei people on the borders of Guizhou, Guangxi and Yunnan Provinces gather from all sides on the Chabai Ground in Xingyi County, to hold the grand Chabai Song Festival.

Chabai is a word formed from the names of a pair of lovers. It is said that the son of a hunter, Chalang who lived on a dam of the Nanpan River, and Baimei, a daughter of a neighboring family fell in love However at that time, a demon tiger appeared in the village creating enormous danger for the people of the community. So Chalang organized all the young men to go out and hunt and kill the tiger. Unfortunately a rich man had also taken a fancy to the young and beautiful Baimei. On the day when Chalang and Baimei were due to get married, he hired an assassin to shoot Chalang with an arrow. The rich man then grabbed Baimei and brought her to his home. Later, Chalang came to rescue Baimei, but was caught by the rich man and killed. In grief Baimei set fire to the rich man's mansion and threw herself into the flames where she perished, choosing death because her love had been taken away from her. The day on which Baimei died for love, June 21, is the day on which the Chabai Song Festival is held.

The Chabai Song Festival mainly involves young people singing antiphonal songs, which are also called "four, six or eight sentences". Most are love songs, in which questions are asked and answered and in which the rhyming rules are very strict. The answering singer must repeat the previous sentence of lyrics sung as his beginning, and produce on the spot his or her own rhyming reply. An inappropriate response can lead to derision and scorn.

The Chabai Song Festival is a large-scale event with over ten thousand participants. It is one of the most important social events of the year for the Bouyei people. They compete in the daytime and at night they sing in their own or their friend's or neighbor's house, where sticky rice dyed in five different colors and rice wine are served for the guests. Many people also visit relatives and friends during the festival, eating stewed dishes, in which a cauldron is used to stew pork. This food is said to originate from the stewing of the tiger killed by Chalang.

The Jianchuan County Shibaoshan Mountain Song Festival celebrated by the Bai Ethnic Minority Group

The Shibaoshan Mountain Songfest celebrated in Jianchuan County by the Bai Ethnic Minority Group is a unique and vivid occasion. Every year during three days between the end of July and the beginning of August according to the lunar calendar, thousands of young Bai people in Jianchuan, Yunlong, Lanping, Heqing and Lijiang County gather at Shizhong Temple, Baoxiang Temple, Haiyun Residence and Jinding Temple on Shibaoshan Mountain to sing their wonderful songs, antiphonal as well as other styles.

The Bai girls taking part in the festival dress up in beautiful clothes, singing long melodious harmonies with their golden voices as they walk to where the festivities will take place. The Bai boys attach a unique sanxian, decorated with a dragon head, to their chest, and playing lilting bright sanxian melodies, as they make their way. Taken together with the sound of Bai love songs mixing with the clear notes of the sanxian, it truly makes for a wonderful scene. The sweet, beautiful and pleasant lyrics commemorate a legendary young and beautiful female singer from 2,000 years ago. The festival gives young people an opportunity to make new friends find a soul mate or lover. At night, in the woods or near the gurgling spring, the young people play sanxian songs to communicate their emotions and feelings. These songs accompanied by the music of the sanxian is a typical courting ritual for the Bai people,

On the Way to the Dong Singing Festival

Most singing and dancing activities are especially associated with particular song festivals, but some which are named after song festivals are connected with other celebrations such as the New Year, ancestor worship and harvest time. Notable examples include the Caigetang, On the Way to the Dong Singing Festival and the Shuagetang Festival of the Yao people.

The Dong are an ethnic minority famed for their singing and dancing. There are more than ten Gange festival grounds in the areas of Tianzhu, Jinping, Jianhe, Sanhui, Zhenyuan in the northeast prefecture of Guizhou Province. The most well known are the Ershiping (Defeat and Victory Slope) Singing Ground of Tianzhuduma, the Shaiyoupo Singing Ground of Bangdong, the Baila'ao Singing Ground of Yutang, the Pingmang Singing Ground of Yunakou, the Shidong Singing Ground of Hanzhai, and the Gaoba Singing Ground at the border of Jinping and Jianhe Counties. The grandest however is the Ershiping Singing Ground of Tianzhuduma. The festival there lasts for three days with between 20 and 30,000 participants.

Song festivals are held in different areas at different times: that of the Ershiping, Gaoba and Shaiyoupo Singing Grounds are, according to the lunar calendar, held each year from July 20 to 22, on July 20 and April 8 respectively.

Each singing ground has its own legend. For example, the Ershiping Singing Ground of Tianzhuduma, is associated with the following legend. Long, long ago, in the area of Ganxi, not far from Duma, a young singer loved singing like a butterfly loves flowers, so he came to be called "Peerless Singer". The young girls of the nearby villages also enjoyed his songs and came to listen. His fame spread far and wide quickly, and increasing numbers of people flocked to hear his marvelous voice. On July 20 of the lunar calendar, a huge crowd of people came and began spontaneously to sing antiphonally with "Peerless Singer". This lasted for three full days and proved so memorable an event that it was repeated each year. In the end Ershiping became quite a busy town. Henceforth the Dong people set aside the three days from June 20 to 22 as a festival for getting together and singing antiphonally. The festival came to be called "On the Way to the Dong Singing Festival."

Every time the festival comes around, no matter the weather, thousands upon thousands of young Dong, Miao, and Han people from Dong Township, which spreads for hundreds of li, congregate at the singing venue and joyfully burst into the full repertoire of Dong songs. Besides the wonderful singing competitions held by the young people, other events are also staged such as bullfights and traditional drama performances.

Shuagetang Festival of the Yao Ethnic Group

The Getang Festival in Liannan and Bapaiyao in the Lianshan area of Guangdong Province is also known as the Shuawang or Shuagetang Festival.

The Shuagetang Festival of the Yao Ethnic Group is usually held around October 16 by the lunar calendar, during the harvest period. Two legends explain the origins of the festival: one sees it as commemorating the great ancestor of the Yao, Dengfabao; the other sees it as expelling ghosts and praying for the safety of the people and the health of their livestock.

The Shuage Festival is principally an occasion on which people pay respects to their ancestors. The old men carry aloft the memorial tablets of their grandfathers and bear them from the temple through the villages while the people respectfully salute. This is also a time when the newly harvested corn, sweet potato, wine, zanba and mountain fruits are also paraded, and the bounty of the harvest is publicly displayed and celebrated. During the period of the festival, every household prepares two or three jin of zanba to offer visiting

friends and relatives, as well as several jin of wine for the enjoyment of the general crowds who congregate for the festivities. After some firecrackers are let off the piercing notes of the cow horn and the echoes of gongs and drums sound through the air, and the young men begin the tambourine dance, as the girls wearing colorful embroidered clothes dance along behind. The people tuck in to the food and chat away happily, or sing aloud traditional Yao Songs amid a scene of joyful hustle and bustle.

The Shoton Festival of the Tibetan Ethnic Group

The Shoton Festival of the Tibetan Ethnic Group is an especially entertaining festival. In Tibetan, 'Shoton' means eating fermented milk. The origin of the festival is very much related to Tibetan Buddhism. Before the 17th century, according to the doctrines of the Gelug sect of Tibetan Buddhism, the time from April 15 to June 30 by the Tibetan Calendar was a period of prohibition, during which, the lamas of the large and small Tibetan temples of Tibet were forbidden to go out for fear of stepping on or killing grass, trees or insects. This was called "Ya le", which in Tibetan, means "Peaceful summer habitation". June 1 by the Tibetan calendar is the day on which the prohibition ends, and lamas traditionally went down the mountain, and their relatives and friends brought fermented milk to welcome them back to the world. Everyone would then drink the milk, dance and sing on the way back home. This activity ultimately evolved into the festival as celebrated today.

As time passed, the activities associated with the festival became more and more colorful, with more and more entertaining activities being incorporated into the festival. The main activity nowadays is traditional Tibetan drama performances. There are twelve Tibetan drama groups who take part in the performances, including the Zaxixueba, Jiongba, Xiangba, JuemuLong, Tazhong, Lunzhugang, Langzewa, Bindunba, Ruoniega, Xirongzhongzi, and Gongbuzhuoba groups. This marvelous festival, which has a history of more than 300 years, is thus also known as the "Tibetan Drama Festival".

The eight traditional Tibetan dramas, which are moral tales encouraging people to do good deeds, have become the main content of the Shoton Festival. One of the most notable, the Dunyue Dunzhu, is an interesting story. Dunzhu was wandering in a foreign country, which was suffering from a terrible drought, and was facing extinction. The people were advised to offer a human sacrifice to the Dragon god and Dunzhu was chosen to be the sacrifice and was taken to the palace. There he fell in love with the princess, and so the king could not bear to go through with killing Dunzhu, even if it meant saving his people. Dunzhu insisted however, placing the needs of the community above his own life. The Dragon god was greatly moved at Dunzhu's great altruism and set him free, bringing rain and good luck to save the people of the land.

CHAPTER VI WOMEN's FESTIVALS

There are many festivals in China which have special relevance for women. In traditional Chinese culture, like many other cultures, women are accorded a subordinate position in society to men. In many ways in traditional patriarchal society, women were, and indeed are, seen as little more than an appendage of men. This has called forth a spirit of rebellion and resistance among many women and this is reflected in many ethnic Chinese festivals.

The Double Seventh Festival, which takes love as its theme, the Sisters Festival, which serves as an occasion for women to get together, the Mid-Autumn Festival, which is associated with reunion and the wonderful Flower-picking Festival, all share a common subject: the pursuit of freedom in one's life. These festivals are a spirited articulation of a longing for pure love, for independence in terms of both family and social life: a statement about the roles women believe they should be allowed to play in society. Women Festivals thus reveal in their customs a vivid and heartfelt appeal for a better life.

In these festivals women of all ethnic groups participate in order to show their own culture's distinctive features. They dance and sing displaying the distinct charms of their own cultures and indeed their own gender at women's festivals like the Sisters Festival of the Yi and the Bai, the Girls' Festival of the Yao and the Daughters' Fair of the Tujia.

I. Enjoying the Sisters' Meal and the Sisters Festival

Enjoying the Sisters' Meal

Beside the Qingshui River which runs across Taijiang and Shibing Counties in southeast Guizhou Province, the women of the Miao ethnic minority celebrate the Sisters Festival. Also known as the festival of "Enjoying the Sisters' Meal", this festival has a rich bank of stories and myths associated with it.

Legend has it that this place in ancient times was a remote backwater and seventy or eighty beautiful girls remained unmarried. In order to make themselves known to the outside world, the 15th day of the 2nd month in spring was chosen as the day on which a festival would be held.

Another story tells of how in the remote past, the festival was held so as to provide a social environment in which young men and women could overcome their shyness and inhibitions, mingle together socially and thus facilitate marriages.

Another legend tells the tale of how the custom of one clan of Taijiang County was to marry off their girls to people outside of the clan. However the girls about to be wed couldn't bear to be parted from their parents and cried:

We all were born to mama and papa,
All were carried on mama's back,
All have slept on mama's bed,
Then why should brothers be so cruel-hearted,
That they must marry us to people from afar?

In order to comfort their daughters, the fathers and mothers decided to celebrate the Sisters Festival, affording brothers and sisters a chance to sing and dance and rejoice together.

Another story speaks of the custom of cousins marrying each other around Shidong. Boys and girls had very little freedom in choosing their own partner. Consequently girls were eager to have a proper occasion on which they could meet and socialize with boys. In the end their mothers organized this festival for just this reason.

In olden times, so another legend goes, in the areas of the Miao, cousins regarded each other as brother and sister and thus marriage among them was prohibited. However, a pair of cousins in Shidong fell in love with each other. The girl Ah Jiao secretly set aside meals for her cousin Jin Dan and eventually they managed to overcome the strictures of society and got married. Later, there were eight hundred girls in the Shidong area who had not found husbands; and coincidentally, there were eight hundred lads who were still bachelors. Old people recalled the story of Ah Jiao and Jin Dan whose love was facilitated by "sharing the sisters' meal"; therefore they adopted this festival as a means to help young people to find their life partners.

The custom of having the sisters' meal has a long history. It is a living reflection of the ancient marriage custom where the people of one clan married the girls of another. It is however also a reflection of the bond between daughters and mothers, and of the daughter's revolt against the traditional marriage system, or their longing for the freedom of choosing their own mate.

The "Sisters' meal" is made by the Miao girls with sticky rice. In the Miao language, it's called "Jia Liang". "Jia" means meal; "Liang" is a kind of shrub that sheds a special fragrance and is said to have the function of warding off mosquitoes. The meal cooked with Liang turns yellow, which makes it not only very good-looking but also very tasty.

For the festival, girls prepare sticky rice in their family homes, steaming it and making it into beautiful yellow colors. When the young men return, the girls put the food in little

bamboo baskets and then present these baskets to the men. At the moment when a boy receives the meal, he will be greatly overjoyed and inspired, for the meal is a token of love from the girl: the two interlinked bamboo hooks of the basket represent the intention of further meetings; a full clove of garlic symbolizes the breaking off of relations; if there are wide leaves or pine needles in the basket, it is an expression of appreciation.

After breakfast the next day, the girls of one village will sing antiphonally with the lads from another village. In this way they try to find out the quality of the family, character, age and interests of their counterparts. These remote villages at this time echo to the beautiful melodies of these happy songs.

Other Festivals Related to Women

Every 4th day of the 2nd month is held the Girls' Festival of the Hani people who live in Yuanyang County, Yunnan Province. The festival owes its origins to a most tragic story: once there was a beautiful girl who fell in love with a handsome hunter. Unfortunately her parents insisted on marrying her off to the son of Tusi (the local governor). Later, the girl, together with three other girls who suffered the same fate, jumped off a cliff to their deaths.

This terrible legend is an illustration of women's determination to pursue their own hearts when it comes to love. During the festival young men borrow some beautiful clothes from the lady that they love. They disguise themselves as girls, and dance together with them, at the same time expressing their love and respect for the girls' loyalty. Married men carry water and firewood home and boil water for their wives to use when bathing. On this day, men shoulder all the responsibilities of doing housework, after which both men and women rejoice together.

The Butterfly Fair which is held beside the Erhai Lake in Dali, Yunnan Province, falls on the 15th day of the 4th lunar month every year and is the time when young men and women exchange sweet sentiments of love and passion. It is said that once Ah Hua, the deft seamstress gave her love, the brave hunter Ah Long, a colorful scarf embroidered with a hundred butterflies. When the king of Dali learned that Ah Hua was not only a beauty of beauties but was also clever and wise, he deceived her into becoming his concubine. On hearing the news, the lovers fled, closely pursued by the king's guards. Trapped and with no hope of escape, the pair of passionate lovers threw themselves into the deep waters of the Butterfly Spring. Suddenly, a gale force wind, stinging rain, accompanied by enormous bursts of thunder and lighting were unleashed on the land and tens of thousands of butterflies poured out of the stream, forming the most dazzling and multicolored swirling, living ribbon on the branches of the trees above the waters of the stream. The

Butterfly Fair beside the Erhai Lake is a commemoration of this wonderful tale of star-crossed lovers.

In the area of Enshi located in the west of Hubei Province, the Daughters' Fair of the Tujia people is held on the 12th day of the 7th lunar month to provide an occasion on which young people can come to know, understand and love each other, and ultimately exchange marriage vows and pledges. Owing to the sparseness of the local population and the close ties of the community, social circles and the opportunity for varied social intercourse available to young people were in the past understandably quite limited. Thus intermarriage, especially between cousins became quite prevalent. Arranged marriage often between quite young children was also very common with child brides held in bondage a regular occurrence. Amid such a sorry situation, the Daughters' Fair evolved as an event at which young people's range of social intercourse with their peers could be extended. It has become a much-loved ritual and has been handed down from generation to generation.

Young men and women express their affection through antiphonal songs; they thus become acquainted and establish a relationship which may continue and develop in the future. The Daughters' Fair is a vital social outlet for a people who live under relatively closed circumstances, and it makes a major contribution towards minimizing intermarriage and the consequent health and social dangers that entails.

The Flower Arrangement Festival held in the Night-blooming Cereus Mountain area of Dayao County, Yunnan Province on the 8th day of the 2nd lunar month is a festival in memory of a girl who sacrificed herself for the sake of saving the community from evil. On this day, people pin flowers to their hair, collect flowers in baskets and carry around flowers. They also build beautiful floral tents where they the festival is celebrated. The dances and love songs of boys and girls are the highlight of the festivities.

The Custom of Beauty Contests

In festivals with special relevance for females, or in festivals celebrated together by both men and women, old and young, the custom of beauty contests is a regular occurrence. In modern terms, such events are effectively equivalent to fashion shows.

The costumes the women from various ethnic groups and areas wear on these occasions are not unique to their own cultural groups and areas, but also are usually made by the girls themselves in elaborate ways. All colors and designs are distinctive and during these festive gatherings, the girls' beautiful clothes bloom gorgeously like exotic flowers.

Liangshan Mountain of Sichun Province is the home of the Yi people. Their well-known Torch Festival is held every year on the 24th day of the 6th month. One story

associated with the festivities tells of the unswerving loyalty of Madam Benevolence, the wife of the head of the Mengshe Zhao (tribe). There are many recreational activities which take place during the Torch Festival. For example, when performing their group dance, the girls eagerly contend with each other to be adjudged the one with the most pleasing voice, steps, costumes, looks, etc. According to the traditional aesthetic tastes of the Yi, a girl with finely arched eyebrows, double-edged eyelids, a high and straight nose, large, black eyeballs, thin lips, a well-proportioned jaw-line and dimpled cheekbones when smiling is held to be the very epitome of beauty. The Yi also attach great importance to inner wisdom and virtue. As the beautiful, virtuous and hardworking girls arrayed in bright-colored costumes pass before the people one after another, they receive heartfelt appreciation and praise from the admiring audience.

The Costume-Embroidering Fair is celebrated every year by the Yi people on the 15th day of the 1st lunar month in the Tanhua Mountain of the Chuxiong Autonomous Prefecture, Yunnan Province. Legend has it that there once was a great hero who arose from among the people. Girls from the local communities all wanted to marry him. The hero loved the mountains and waters of his hometown very much, so he said he would marry whichever girl could embroider best the mountains and waters on clothes. In order to be the wife of such a hero, the maids all strived to embroider beautiful clothes, and this event inspired the establishment of this traditional festival. On this day, the girls all put on their flowery hats, clothes, and shoes, and in groups congregate on the grassland to sing and dance, all of which provides a dazzling display for the local lads!

II. Mid-Autumn Festival and Women

"When Mid-Autumn Festival arrives, the moon appears especially round"; in the blue-black sky, a golden round moon casts its clear light on the land, which arouses people limitless yearning. As this is the time for harvesting crops, the Mid-Autumn Festival assumes much importance in people's lives. Ethnic minority groups such as Tujia, Dai, Maonan, Jing, Dong, Man, Yi, Ewenki, Oroqen, and Korea Ethnic Minority Group all have special ways of celebrating the event.

Mid-Autumn Festival is on August 15 of the lunar calendar, and although it is a national festival, in some areas, the custom that "males don't worship the moon and the female don't offer sacrifices to the kitchen god" still exists so that date has a close relationship with Chinese women.

The story about the Moon Goddess, Chang'e, is included in ancient Chinese legends where she is referred to as a "Moon Spirit". Ancient humans believed in perpetual rejuvenation and bringing the dead back to life on the moon and water, and then connected this concept to the menses of women, and calling it "monthly water". The Zhuang Ethnic Group also has an ancient fable, saying that the sun and moon are a couple and the stars are their children, and when the moon is pregnant, it becomes round, and then becomes crescent after giving birth to a child, hence, the moon and women form an indissoluble bond.

On Mid-Autumn Festival, it is popular for women to worship and offer sacrifices to the moon.

Korean women residing at the foot of Changbaishan Mountain have the custom of welcoming the moon. When the gentle night falls, they put up a high and large conical house frame with dry pine branches and called a "moon house". When the moon rises, the moon house is lit up, forming a bright and dazzling torch, and the people fall over each other to be the first to see the moon, which is considered great good luck. While the full moon hangs high in the sky, the women dressed in their best step on the springboard, as light as swallows or like butterflies.

The women of Guangzhou area have the custom of lifting up lanterns, which are framed by thin bamboo strips and then pasted with oilpaper on the surface. The colorful lanterns vary in styles, some like glittering fruits, some lively and vigorous, some flying like frightened geese, and some like flying dragon, full of beauty and in riotous profusion. At night, the people lift the lanterns on the eaves or in another high place, thus looking like stars to welcome the bright moon.

There are also many ethnic groups where the women rather offer sacrifices to the moon. Under the glittering moon in the still night sky, the people place a table in the courtyard, on the flat roof or near the yard door, with various sacrifices placed on it such as moon cakes, guavas, chestnuts, candies and alcoholic drinks and so on. Old women officiate over the worship ceremony. The Bouyei Ethnic Group calls the Mid-Autumn Festival "Worshiping Moon Festival", and in this month, every household makes glutinous new rice cakes and sticky rice, first worshiping the ancestors and then dining together. At night, the glutinous new rice cake is brought to the doorway to worship the Moon Grandmother. The ceremony of the Tu Ethnic Group is called "Beating the Moon", that is placing a basin of clear water in the courtyard, letting the inverted image of the moon appear in the water and then beating the water surface with branches. In the Maonan Ethic Group, they tie a bamboo pole near the table, about one or two *zhang* long,

on which a grapefruit is hung, with also three lit incense sticks on it. This is called "Shooting the Moon".

The Yi Ethnic Group, distributed in the areas of Yunnan Province and so on, holds a Taiyin Fair at night when the moon is bright, with the old women as active participants. While worshiping, they write the characters of "Taiyin Bodhisattva" on yellow paper and offer plain food and fruits as sacrifices.

After worshiping and offering sacrifices to the moon, they share out the moon cakes. The moon cakes, a vital part of the celebration, vary in size between different areas, and are divided into two kinds, with crisp or hard surface, and with various stuffing materials. The moon cake symbolizes the full moon and means reunion in the world. Women in China largely take it meaning reunion and safety. In olden times, if the women would like to return to her parents' home for a while, they had to return to their husband's home on August 15. So the Mid-Autumn Festival is called Reunion Festival, and some people still call the moon cake as "Reunion Cake" even now. The areas of Zhejiang and Fujian provinces in olden times named the moon cakes in Mazu Temple as "Getting Rich Cake" to pray for becoming rich.

The Dong Ethnic Group living in the Guizhou Area has the custom of "Moon Celebrating" together. The girls of Zu Village should sing "Way Blocking Songs", and the hostess should sing "Toast Songs" when entertaining the guests and "Farewell Songs" for sending them off and so on. The Dong Ethnic Group residing in the area of Xinhuang and other parts of Hunan Province has the custom of Stealing Moon Vegetables. Every time the Mid-Autumn Festival arrives, the women use an umbrella to hide themselves and pick up some token melon and fruit from another person's field, specially the twinned beans and those on one stalk, and after it, they call loudly the name of the owner, saying: "I have picked your fruits, and you can come to my home to eat fried flour!" The Zhuang Ethnic Group has the custom of "Scolding Mid-Autumn Festival" when young people especially play some tricks involving scolding.

In Daguang, in the Nanming area of the Miao and Dong Autonomous Prefecture in the northeast of Guizhou Province, the people of the Dong Ethnic Group hold Mid-Autumn Festival in special flavor. The girls and young men make an appointment at a certain place and usually the girls arrive early and overhear the remarks about them being made by the young men; but the latter are unaware of this and if one is careless to make an inappropriate remark and hurt the girl's feelings, it will damage the sentiment. Most of the young men wisely praise their lovers in front of their fellows, and the listening girls then walk out of the thicket. Pairs of lovers then go off to a quiet place to open their hearts

to each other.

The Mid-Autumn Festival of the Jing Ethnic Group has also content of courting, but in more witty style. As the bright moon rises up in the sky and the antiphonal songs help them find each other is congenial company, they take out prepared flower shoes to match, and if the shoes form a pair, it means "Heaven-made match", and then they use each other's shoe and to beat and create a rhythm for the love songs and dances.

In many areas, the women steal melon to pray for having child, and the Tujia Ethnic Group, call August 15 Stealing Melon Festival.

III. Flowers-Picking Festival

The florescent season is charming, and the flowers are the symbol of beauty, as well as a special pronoun for the female. Many traditional festivals of each ethnic group and area are special for women, amid which Flowers-Picking Festival is most often featured.

The Flowers-Picking Festival is widely distributed throughout the country among groups such as Tibetan, Qiang, Miao, Dong, Bai, Gaoshan, Mongolia and Daur Ethnic Groups.

Although each group adds some distinctive features the Flowers-picking Festival are largely identical, combining folk-customs and some folklore, with many women participating together, festively singing and dancing together.

As for the festival, the Tibetans have a beautiful legend. The Boyu Area was originally a remote and backward place, in which it was difficult for the people to live. One day, a beautiful girl called Lianzhi came there and taught people to open up the wasteland, spin and weave and pick flowers to cure illness. However, on May 5 one year, when caught in a bad storm, the girl froze to death under the flowery tree on the snow-covered mountain. In order to commemorate her, the people established the Flowers-picking Festival, on which the girls pick up flowers with songs, with many especially for Lianzhi.

The Flowers-picking Festival is held on the Fourth and Fifth day of May in the lunar calendar every year by Tibetan women in the Boyu area of Wen County in Gansu Province. In the early morning, wearing new clothes and carrying delicious food, the girls go to the mountain to pick the wild flowers together, singing antiphonally and happily in a loud voice, and frolicking and chasing each other. When they arrive at their chosen place, they scatter to pick flowers while continuing to sing. The songs fill the mountains, as well as the sea of flowers, to create a magical environment. Bathed in the dense fragrance of the

flowers which the wind cannot disperse and the spacious wild cannot contain, the Tibetan girls project their loud and clear voices, merging the physical beauty of the women, natural beauty of the wild flowers and the artistic beauty of music and creating a world of sincerity, kindness and beauty. At dusk, everyone sit around the campfire, singing throughout the night, the flames reddening the girls' faces.

On the following morning, the girls put the flowers in their hair, or make a ring of flowers, and make ready to return with more melodious songs. When entering the village, the children go to welcome them with food, and the flowers-picking army walks and sings hand in hand. Finally, the girls give flowers to every household in the village.

The Gaoshan Ethnic Group living on Taiwan Island for generations also has its own Flowers-picking Festival, generally the same as that of Tibetan Ethnic Group. The Gaoshan are good at singing and dancing, and on the Flowers-picking Festival, the girls wear new clothes and put on a ring of flowers, singing and dancing as much as they like.